Creative Parenting After Separation

Elizabeth Seddon is a social worker/family therapist who has worked in the area of family relationships for many years. She was Director of Relationships Australia, Canberra and Region for twelve years and more recently was National Director of Relationships Australia. She is presently an Honorary Research Fellow in the Department of Social Policy, University of Edinburgh and the Centre for Research on Family and Relationships at the same university. She also works as a family counsellor in Scotland. She has personal experience of parenting after separation and coping with the challenges of living in a stepfamily.

Creative Parenting After Separation

Elizabeth Seddon

For my father and mother,
Joe and Nancy.

First published in 2003

Allen & Unwin
83 Alexander Street
Crows Nest NSW 2065
Australia
Phone: (61 2) 8425 0100
Fax: (61 2) 9906 2218
Email: info@allenandunwin.com
Web: www.allenandunwin.com

National Library of Australia
Cataloguing-in-Publication entry:

Seddon, Elizabeth I.
Creative parenting after separation: a happier way forward.

Bibliography.
Includes index.
ISBN 1 74114 049 8.
ISBN 1 74114 149 4 (export edition).

1. Divorced parents. 2. Children of divorced parents.
3. Joint custody of children. 4. Single-parent families.
I. Title.

306.89

Set in 10.5/13 pt Sabon by Bookhouse, Sydney
Printed by Griffin Press, South Australia

10 9 8 7 6 5 4 3 2 1

Contents

Acknowledgments

Many people have contributed to the writing of this book. I want to express my deep gratitude and appreciation to them. Susan Gribbon, Sue Fyvel and Kerrie James read and critiqued my work at different stages of the writing process, offering numerous comments and insights. Bruce Smyth and Ruth Weston from the Australian Institute of Family Studies were incredibly helpful and offered me a new way of talking about the language of separation and a fresh eye. Many of the ideas in this book were informed by my work in this area with David Jones, a colleague during my time at Relationships Australia. Other colleagues at Relationships Australia, Canberra and Region, have also contributed to this book through their willingness to work together to develop innovative ways of assisting couples and families. I wish to thank them also.

I would also like to acknowledge the help and support of the Centre for Research on Families and Relationships at Edinburgh

University where I have had much needed administrative and practical assistance, plus a room in which to write.

I owe a personal debt to my husband, Frank Castles. I am essentially a marriage and family therapist. This book was a new endeavour for me. Frank commented meticulously on the structure and ideas in this book. His ideas, suggestions and support were invaluable and I learnt much from him about the art of writing. Finally, I want to acknowledge our children who taught me so much about parenting after separation and living in a stepfamily.

I gratefully acknowledge the authors and publishers who granted permission to reprint material from works in copyright. Every effort has been made to trace all the other copyright holders but if any have been inadvertently overlooked the publisher will be pleased to make the necessary acknowledgement at the first available opportunity.

1

What is creative parenting all about?

Most parents who are in the process of separating, or thinking about separating, are anxious to do the best by their children. They want to minimise harm and provide a positive environment in which to nurture their children's growth and development. But separating couples often argue over what this means, one or both of them believing that they alone know what is in their children's best interests. Sometimes, the arguments are fuelled by anger, bitterness and grief over the ending of the relationship; at other times, parents are motivated by a genuine but misguided concern about what is best for the children. Occasionally, there is genuine cause for concern about one parent's capacity to care adequately for the children. This continual argument and conflict about what is best for the children often creates the very environment the parents are trying to avoid—one that is fraught with conflict and divided loyalties, with the potential to cause emotional distress to their children.

Although this scenario is quite common, we all know of other couples who manage to part in a different way. While angry and upset over the separation and frequently blaming each other, they manage to put these feelings aside as they negotiate caring and parenting responsibilities for their children. Their children are often consulted about their needs and shielded as much as possible from their parents' conflicts. This allows the children to get on with their own lives, eventually enabling the parents to get on with theirs. With time, some of these parents may even develop a friendship although this isn't necessary for their parenting arrangement to work. These parents are able to work together creatively in an active way. They seek out resources to help them achieve their goals and they handle the inevitable stresses of the situation in a way that creates as much of a win–win situation as is possible for all.

How do some couples manage to separate in a way that allows everyone to get on with their lives in a positive manner, while others spend years wrangling and arguing? What contributes to some parents losing or not maintaining involvement in their children's lives, often losing contact entirely, or playing only a minimal role, distressing the children and leaving them worried and concerned about whether their absent parent really does love and care for them? What is going on in some parents who try to exclude the other parent from the child's life? What about relationships where there has been violence or there is the continuing threat of violence?

Are the needs of children and parents grossly at odds during separation? What prevents parents from acting in ways that will contribute to a positive separation for everybody? What does a positive separation look like? How does separation affect grandparents and other family members? What about repartnering? These are a few of the questions explored in this book.

Why place so much emphasis on the needs of children? We

now know a lot about the potentially detrimental impact of separation and divorce on children; we know that, in the short term, children are distressed and upset by their parents' separation. In the long term, their emotional growth and development, their educational and social opportunities, are influenced by how their parents handle this transition. We know that children exposed to ongoing conflict and caught up in divided loyalties are more at risk of lowered well-being generally.[1]

Separation is frequently followed by a period of economic hardship which can translate into poverty for some children. This is particularly true of children from families where only one parent was working or where the income of two parents was needed to sustain the household before separation. Poverty is linked to lower educational attainment for children, an increased chance of delinquency, more psychological disturbances and the likelihood of reduced earnings as adults.[2]

For the most part, what children need to help them make the transition to a new kind of family lies in the hands of their parents. Whether the conflict continues depends on the type of relationship the parents develop with each other after separation; whether there is severe economic hardship or poverty depends on how child support and income maintenance are arranged. So, it is important that, during and after separation and divorce, parents are aware of the risk factors that could lead to negative outcomes for children so that they can take steps to minimise them.

But because all families are different and each marriage or relationship unique, parents can be creative in the way they build their future relationship with each other and with their children. Many of the old ways of handling separation are counterproductive for children and parents. This is where creativity comes in. Both parents have an opportunity to build a relationship that will work for them and their children, rather than having decisions imposed by courts or dictated by outdated beliefs about marriage that no longer correspond with reality.

Knowing the risk factors and working out what to do about

them is often not sufficient. It's a big jump from knowing what to do to being able to do it—to build a constructive parenting relationship together. Creative parenting after separation depends on two people cooperating at a time when they feel least capable of doing so. For some separating couples it seems that, no matter how hard they try to cooperate with each other, the next encounter brings more conflict. Or one partner may be more capable of co-operating than the other.

The reality is that creative parenting after separation depends on the goodwill of both parents and, if one parent is less cooperative than the other, this can be an obstacle.

Thus, a key focus in this book is on the things that seem to stop parents from forming creative parenting relationships after separation, on the assumption that being able to identify these factors will free parents to move forward. Once parents understand the obstacles and have eliminated them, or learnt how to go round them, they can implement some of the skills and practices that will facilitate the development of a creative parenting relationship.

As separation and divorce becomes more acceptable in our society, it is important that we find a blueprint for it that supports the best outcomes for both adults and children. It is fairly clear that we have not yet done this. We are referring here to marriage and non-marital relationships. The latter are increasing with many children now being born to cohabiting couples. These parents have exactly the same parental responsibilites towards their children after separation. Our society seems to have a very ambivalent attitude towards separation and divorce. We no longer assign legal fault or blame but divorce is still frowned upon socially and we seek to discover which partner was 'at fault'.

Many of our personal attitudes and beliefs, as well as the general beliefs in society, result in separations and divorces that are acrimonious and destructive for all concerned. For children, these separations are profoundly disturbing. They probably reinforce society's ambivalence about separation, because the process of separation doesn't seem to resolve the issues for some parents. In some situations, it actually seems to set in train a whole new load of problems and conflicts.

The debate about separation in our culture has split into opposing camps and is often clouded by ideological thinking. The terms of this debate have a major impact on separating parents because they influence how they think and feel about themselves and their family during the process. Current thoughts about separation also influence how others in the family respond to the separating couple and what advice and support is offered to them. The debate can be summarised as follows:[3]

Many researchers and social commentators see separation as the cause of numerous social evils. It is said that it increases family poverty, weakens ties between the generations, increases child delinquency and educational and mental health problems, and isolates men from their fathering roles. At the extreme, separated people and those contemplating separation are labelled selfish, individualistic and inconsiderate of their children's needs. They are seen to be putting their own needs before those of their children. Cohabitation also poses problems, as it is seen to devalue marriage and make couples more vulnerable to separation.

According to this view, the cure for all these ills is to restrict divorce by making it less available and discourage cohabitation. This would make people take marriage more seriously and work at their relationships. Some even suggest the return of fault-based divorce. They believe that the structure of relationships is the most important element in raising happy and healthy children and that the best structure in which to do this is the intact family.

Other researchers and commentators contend that divorce is one of the greatest liberating forces of our time as it frees people from personally damaging family relationships, dominated by power, conflict, violence and inequality. Supporters of this side of the argument point to the fact that marriage has traditionally depended on women's subordination and on the maintenance of separate spheres for men and women. They see much more potential for happier and more equal relationships today.

They argue that it is not so much the structure of relationships that is important to children, but the quality and consistency of those relationships. Children can and do thrive in a diversity of family structures. Marriages and relationships that are dominated by conflict, violence or fear are far more destructive for children than divorce and separation. The remedy, from this perspective, is to deal with the economic consequences of divorce by supporting single-parent families.

This is not a book about which side of the debate is correct. We are more interested in how attitudes and beliefs arising from the debate influence parents decisions and actions during separation and, ultimately, the shape of the parenting relationship after separation. Both sides of the debate have some merit. Very few people would argue with the proposition that it is simpler and more economically viable for children to be brought up with their natural parents living together. Most research shows that children who start out living with both their parents are, on average, better off both psychologically and financially when raised with those parents. Most parents and children, when asked, ideally want this type of arrangement. Most parents would have preferred their relationship to work.

But there have always been happy and unhappy marriages and the outcomes for children living in unhappy families is just as clear, particularly those families where there are high levels of marital conflict. In these situations, divorce and single-parent households may be better for the children than living with both parents. And, while divorce may provide a gateway to freedom for women in oppressive relationships, for many women it is also a gateway into poverty and a different type of oppression. For men, separation and divorce frequently bring with them the risk of poorer physical and mental health, as well as a fracturing of relationships with their children.

It is clear that nothing much is achieved by reducing the issue to a 'good' versus 'bad' debate. Things are more complex than that. We have to find new ways of helping to sustain relationships and new ways of disentangling them when they are not working.

Many of the ideas in this book were developed in my work as a marriage and family therapist. They are also based on the vast body of findings by researchers in the field of family relationships. These findings go back over 30 years and include a number of long-term studies on the impact of divorce on children. This is a book about how relationships work and about understanding the process of separation. It is not a 'how-to' book. I am seeking to help people make sense of their relationships and their experience of separation, while organising things in a way that best meets the needs of their children. Many parents have told me that guidance on how to build a parenting relationship after separation doesn't really help without some understanding of why their relationships fell apart and how they can be mended. That is what this book tries to do.

Most separating couples do not take the decision to separate lightly. For some, the decision comes after a long struggle to improve their relationship. It may be taken jointly, but more often it is instigated by only one of the partners. In some relationships, separation comes as a surprise because one of the partners may not have realised the extent of the difficulties. For others, separation coincides with the discovery of an affair and is accompanied by overwhelming feelings of being used, deceived and betrayed. Sometimes, the separation marks an escape from an abusive relationship. Other couples vacillate between living separately and reuniting many times over.

Because each situation is unique, couples will arrive at very different solutions about their post-separation arrangements. What is important is what works for them. This is the creative part of the process and involves each individual taking responsibility for arriving at a solution that will work for both the children and the parents in the long term. Despite the uniqueness of each situation, we know there are certain modes of interaction that are better than others in helping to establish a firm foundation for ongoing cooperation. This cooperation is vital when children are involved in the separation.

Over the years I have worked with many people going through the experience of separation and it is clear to me that there are many common themes and struggles in people's experiences. In particular, people's beliefs about marriage and the way they construct the reasons for their separation seem to shape how they respond to their former partner in separation. Many people are caught up in the same cycle. It is only when they take a closer look at those beliefs that they are able to change their attitudes and begin to work in a more cooperative and creative way with the other parent. The scenarios in this book reflect these people's stories. They highlight particular themes but none bears any detailed resemblance to real individuals.

I owe a debt of gratitude to the many people I have seen for allowing me to witness their struggle and for teaching me much of what I now know about the subject. Most importantly, they taught me that, once the path of separation has been embarked upon, parents have to leave their intimate relationship in the past and not allow it to influence their future parenting relationship. This is easier said than done. It is very hard to put aside one's emotions and not let them affect how we behave towards the other parent, now and in the future. Also, people change after they separate. While for some parents the change might be positive for their parenting relationship, for others the change has a negative impact. Parents therefore not only have to cope with emotions from the past, but also emotions that may have their roots in the present.

They also taught me that we must search for solutions that work in the long run for all family members—children, mothers, fathers and grandparents. It is not good enough to make one family member the scapegoat and exclude them from the family. They taught me that solutions that seem to work for children, ultimately also seem to work for parents.

Far from separation and divorce meaning that it is all over, they showed me that it can be a transition towards a new way of relating that preserves relationships for children and the wider family. They also taught me that children can tell us more about what they need than we often give them credit for, but that it is important not to overburden children with too much responsibility for decision making. Once children have begun to recover from the initial impact of their parents' decision to separate, they often come up with solutions that surprise their parents.

Finally, they taught me that, in those families where domestic violence and abuse have been significant issues, we must search for different ways of resolving matters. Cooperation depends on building trust and confidence in each other as parents and this is often not feasible in such situations. While it is usually in the interests of children to maintain a relationship with both parents, there are some important exceptions. Where there is continued violence and abuse, and children fear a parent, it is important to assess the wisdom of further contact. Safety issues are important. Children may be reluctant to see a parent because of past experiences which have left them fearful. Their fear may be the result of direct violence or abuse towards them or it may be a consequence of witnessing violence towards their mother. Sometimes mothers need protection, and contact can be an opportunity for the father to continue harassment and intimidation.

We touch on issues of violence and abuse in this book but the main focus is on building cooperative parenting. It is advisable for parents and children who are trying to sort out a safe separation to seek professional help to assess levels of safety and future possibilities for family relationships.

2

Creative parenting after separation: Does it matter?

A good starting point for exploring why it matters to have creative parenting after separation is to look at what researchers are saying about the impact of separation and divorce on children. As we look at this research, we come to understand why it is worth experimenting with creative ways of redesigning traditional parenting relationships after separation.

In the last 30 years, we have seen a steady growth in this type of research. As with much social research, there are no simple answers. In his book *Men, Mateship and Marriage* Don Edgar points out:

> whereas the early work on divorce effects on young children used small samples to prove that one-parent families caused delinquency, crime and teenage pregnancy, the better work of later years compared them with children from 'intact' families.

> It showed that children, whether from intact or divorced homes, who experienced parental conflict were damaged. It also showed many divorced families could be better off and their children could thrive. But this was often distorted to justify divorce as a good thing.[1]

Separation and divorce have varying effects on families so it is difficult to talk about them as all good or all bad. Sometimes, separation helps to resolve an unbearable relationship situation and make it possible for a couple to lead more positive lives. In other cases, it starts a process that keeps the parents locked in continual conflict and litigation, with deeply disturbing consequences for the children. But not all family members respond in the same way, and it is crucial to take this into account. Not all separations are mutual and children have little say in the process.

Research on separation is now seeing it as part of a process. This process can sometimes begin years before the separation, setting off a chain of events that can have an influence on individuals long after the separation has been finalised.[2] This research gives us many clues about the needs of children before, during and after separation.

We look at two aspects of the separation and divorce research—first, the immediate impact of separation on children, and then the long-term outcomes for children.

Listening to children's stories

Paying attention to what children have to say about separation is quite a new departure in family research. It is even more novel in legal, counselling and mediation practice. Separation and divorce have mainly been seen as 'adults' business'—although children are affected by it, they generally have not had a voice or an influencing role in the process. We have not thought that adults might listen to or be influenced by them in the decisions they might make.

Until recently, separation was something that was done 'to' children, like going to the dentist and having a tooth pulled. However, in 1991 Australia ratified the United Nations Convention on the Rights of the Child, in which children are seen to have rights and interests that need protection. It is more usual now for courts and other public institutions to take children's interests into account in the diverse situations that make up separation and divorce.

Important spin-offs of the UN Convention have been more research into children's experience of separation and developments in the fields of law, counselling and mediation that allow children's voices to be heard when decisions are being made about their welfare. We now see children as capable of holding opinions and participating in decisions that affect their lives. Of course, not everyone shares this view of children's capacities and we discuss this in subsequent chapters. At the moment research is trying to tease out what children think and feel about the impact of separation on their lives.

As with most adults, children experience separation as a time of distress. If you listen to children's stories about separation, some report relief but most talk about it as a time of confusion, sadness, fear and loneliness. Many have ambivalent feelings. Some talk about feelings of guilt and the need to take sides with one parent or the other. They have 'conflicting loyalties' often feeling caught in the middle. When we reflect on children's stories, we see that how children feel is not all that different from how their parents feel.

But what are these feelings about?

Family is central for children

Children feel confused because it is difficult to make sense of their parents' behaviour, their own feelings and the changes that are happening in their lives. They feel sad because they are trying to come to terms with the loss of their family, as they understand it. Young children seem to hold traditional views of family life—they see families as 'consisting of two married parents who live with each other and their children in the same house'.[3] However, children also say that families are about love, mutual respect, care and support.[4] Children who hold this more traditional view of the family have to adjust their mindset if they are to make a successful adjustment to separation.

Children are often fearful and anxious about separation because they are trying to make sense of what is going to happen to them in the future. They are particularly concerned about whether one parent or both might be lost from the family. Some children describe the loss of daily contact with one parent, usually the father, as one of the most devastating aspects of separation. They say they miss their father and are distressed by fathers who are unreliable about their contact visits—the 'no show' dad.[5]

The act of separation also seems to come as a shock to many children, even if they have heard their parents talk about it. This seems to be true even in homes where violence and conflict is a way of life. Children from high-conflict families, when asked how they feel about the separation, often express ambivalent feelings of both 'relief and sadness'.[6] Some children from violent families may want the violence to stop, but they may not see separation as a means of achieving this. Others are relieved at being released from living in fear. Generally, children take their family as the fundamental basis of their life, their source of security and survival. Separation is an immediate threat to this security. Researchers point out:

> At the time of parental separation, the child's attention is riveted on his or her own family, and he is intensely worried about what is going to happen to him. Whatever its shortcomings, the family is perceived by the child at this time as having provided the support and protection he needs. Divorce signifies the collapse of that structure and he feels very alone and frightened.[7]

Children feel isolated

Children often feel lonely because they are unsure about whether it is right to discuss the situation with their parents and other people. Some children feel their parents are less available to them after separation, perhaps because the parents are severely distressed.[8] Some children fear that talking about their own distress will increase their parents' distress and will try to protect their parents from having to handle their child's unhappiness as well.[9] Some children feel conflicting loyalties because they love both their parents and are sensitive to any hint of blame from one towards the other. Many children believe they have to take a position on the rights and wrongs of what is going on, even if this is not actually demanded of them by their parents. Feeling caught in the middle, some children are not able to talk about the situation with either parent.

Some children feel guilty, believing they are in some way responsible for the separation, particularly if they have witnessed or overheard parents fighting about them. This feeling of guilt can increase their sense of isolation from their parents.

Hearing about the separation

Of particular interest is the number of children who say they do not know *why* their parents separated. One recent research study in Britain revealed these findings:[10]

- 32 per cent of children said they were given some explanation but without details or the opportunity to ask questions;
- 45 per cent said they were told about the separation in a harsh way with no explanation;
- only 5 per cent felt they had been given a full explanation and positively 'encouraged to ask questions'.

This limited communication between parents and children is worrying. Good explanation and support for children by their parents at the time of separation are important factors influencing their adjustment.

This same study found that children saw grandparents as very important sources of emotional support during the early stages of separation. Depending on the age of the child, friends also played a prominent support role.

It would be easy to assume that from these findings that many parents are uncaring about their children. But the experience of family therapy suggests that this is not the case. There are several possible explanations. Telling their children about their decision to part is one of the most challenging aspects of the separation for many parents. They worry about their children's reactions and they are concerned about their capacity to handle their own emotions. Many parents want to shield their children from their distress and so telling their children about the separation comes out in a peremptory way. Parents' efforts to remain unemotional and calm in front of their children may also contribute to children remaining quiet and not pursuing further explanations, long after the separation has taken place.

It is also clear that many parents just do not know what to say to their children. There is a big discrepancy between what they feel are the real reasons for the separation and what they feel they can reasonably tell their children. Many parents rightly resist the urge to blame each other in front of the children, but as a result their capacity to talk to their children seems to be diminished. This leads to some children finding it difficult to understand why their parents are separating.

If they are given the real reasons for the separation, they may find it difficult to understand them. Or it is hard for them to accept the simplified but inherently unbelievable reasons that parents sometimes offer, because they do not seem serious enough. They are not sure whether the separation is really necessary, particularly if parents have hidden their difficulties from them. Children may find it hard to believe that serious difficulties exist that cannot be overcome, or they may think their parents have not made serious attempts to sort out the trouble.

There can also be a discrepancy between children's experience of what their parents are saying and what the parents *think* their children are hearing. Explanations may be set out in such a way that the child does not understand the reasons for the separation, or what is going to happen as a result. Children also learn to shield themselves.

And yet the message from children is clear. If we listen to what they actually tell us, we find that many of them learn about their parents' separation in a way that is bewildering and distressing for them. This is particularly so if they find out after one parent has already left, or if they are told in an angry manner that blames the other parent.

An emotional gap

Separation frequently only becomes real to children when one of their parents leaves the family home. Given that the family represents children's source of security, it is not uncommon for children to fantasise about keeping the family together in various ways. However, children usually have very little control over the outcome. Their lack of power in the situation contributes to their fear and overall confusion. Many researchers and counsellors comment that some children and parents seem to 'get out of whack' at this stage of the process. Children want the family to stay together and fear what is going to happen, while many adults are ready to move on, wanting to put the past behind and build a new life. These parents may want their children to react in the same way as themselves, although children, understandably, are in a different space.

Disturbed behaviour

Many children in the early stages of parental separation exhibit emotional and behavioural disturbances. These behaviours are a result of the child's confusion, fear, sadness and anger. Some children develop attachment anxieties, as a result of their fear of being separated from one or both parents.

It is crucial to understand the nature of children's attachment.[11] As babies, we develop attachment bonds with our parents and they with us. This attachment forms the basis of our future close relationships. We learn to feel secure, loved and nurtured. Young babies who are adequately fed but receive no affection fail to thrive. Children who feel secure in their attachment are able to venture out and explore the world. They feel safe in their relationships and are thus more confident in their own abilities.

The nature of children's attachment changes with their age. If they have received consistent affection and care and have developed a secure base, they will, as they grow older, use this base to become more independent. They will tend to find others trustworthy and be able to develop satisfying personal relationships. Separation and divorce may threaten children's attachment and it is not unusual to find that most children exhibit some form of behavioural disturbance at first. This behavioural change is a sign of the child's anxiety.

How children behave in response to feeling anxious varies enormously. Some may become withdrawn while others may 'act out' more. They may start to fail at school, become more difficult to manage at home or regress to earlier, immature behaviour. Many children become 'clingy' or aggressive. Most of these behaviours diminish as children come to grips with their new lives. It is important to regard their initial behavioural responses as a normal reaction to the fact of family transition. It would be surprising if children did not have some concerns or display some kind of disruptive behaviour.

Helping children to cope

How to manage their children's immediate response to separation is a concern for many parents. Early on in the process, children need reassurance to relieve them of anxiety and uncertainty about their future and the future of their relationships within the family. If they get this reassurance, they seem to be remarkably resilient. However, if children's uncertainty and anxiety are not attended to but perpetuated by exposure to continued conflict or by the loss of one parent, then separation may place them more at risk.

Talking to children about the separation, explaining the reasons for it in simple terms and encouraging them to ask questions whenever they feel the need is very important. Giving children reassurance and being available to listen to their concerns also helps, and so does encouraging them to talk to other family members and friends. Letting children know that you understand how they feel while, at the same time, not accepting disruptive and antisocial behaviour is a strategy that works for many parents. Children seem to respond positively to firm structure at this time, even though it is often difficult for parents to maintain firm control because they are feeling distressed and are preoccupied with other issues themselves.

Finally, minimising conflict, sorting out living arrangements as soon as possible and setting a plan in place whereby children know they will have a continuing relationship with both parents are all crucial ways of resolving children's initial reactions to a separation. They reassure children they will not be abandoned, they calm their fears and enable them to re-establish some certainty in their lives.

Parents' ability to manage their children's responses in a productive way can be limited by a number of factors. Although separation may not come as a surprise to either parent, one of the parents may feel abandoned in the same way that the children do. They may unwittingly reinforce their children's fears and confusion, particularly if the 'abandoned' partner attacks and blames the other for all their current difficulties. In this situation, children may feel forced to take sides. It is also fertile ground for parents to blame everything that happens from this point onwards, particularly the child's behaviour, on the other parent or on the separation itself.

Sometimes, one or both parents underestimate how deeply the experience is affecting their children. One possible explanation for this is that parents are protecting themselves. No parents like to think that their decisions are causing their children distress. Parents may feel guilty about their decision to separate and this guilt gets in the way of relating to their children. One response is to deny or underestimate their children's feelings and reactions to the situation.

It may also be that parents are less available to their children, both physically and emotionally, at the time of separation. Some parents are preoccupied and overwhelmed by their own separation issues. They may be in a state of shock, depressed, irritable, angry, unpredictable or just plain tired from trying to reorganise their lives.

Other parents are preoccupied with new relationships. A new partner or prospective partner engages their attentions and emotions. This often bewilders children who may feel that the object of their affection—their parent—has been 'captured' by another person. Some children may experience this as rejection. The presence of a new partner can also contribute to a former partner's difficulty in managing anger and blame, particularly if the cause of separation is identified with the beginning of a new intimate relationship for the other parent, or with deception about an affair. Some children may appear to be coping well but, when we look more closely, we can see that they are focused on looking after the vulnerable parent—in essence, they have become the responsible adult. These children have no room to attend to their own experiences.

Changes after change

Separation may bring with it other changes to children's lives. There may be a change of residence and schools; with this comes loss of contact with old friends and extended family members; relationships must be formed with new people. They may need to live with one parent's new partner or step-sibling. Children may find they have less access to material possessions and other resources as a result of reduced family income. These are challenging issues for children to deal with.

Matthew's situation (see box) illustrates many common issues for children at separation.

> Katrina brought Matthew, aged 11, to counselling because she was concerned about his behaviour. She and Matthew's father had separated four months before. Matthew lives with his mother. Katrina has recently formed a new relationship, although her new partner does not live with her. Matthew found out about the separation by being told that his father had moved out. This came as a surprise to him, although he had heard his mum and dad fighting a lot. He has not talked much with his mum about the separation. At first, he saw his dad every weekend but this has become less regular and more unpredictable. He has not had an explanation of the separation from his dad. His dad now has a girlfriend, whom Matthew says he quite likes.
>
> Katrina is concerned that Matthew is doing less well at school, has become more aggressive, and is rude and disobedient to both her and her new partner. She is yelling at him more and says she is at her wits' end. Matthew is now saying he wants to live with his dad. As I talked and played with Matthew, he expressed his sadness about the separation and his hope that his mum and dad would get back together again. He wanted his mum's new partner to go away and he was afraid that he would not see his real dad nearly as much. As we talked more it became clear that Matthew blamed his mum's new partner for his parents' separation.

Katrina has already worked out that much of what is happening with Matthew is related to the separation but she is at a loss to know how to handle it. She does not find it easy to talk to Mathew or to encourage him to talk about the separation. She feels guilty about the separation and has been somewhat overindulgent of Matthew since his father left. On the other hand, she often feels very angry with him when he is defiant and will not do as he is asked.

Katrina decided to insist on better behaviour from Matthew and follow through with consequences. She also determined to talk to him about the separation and let him know that she understands that it is difficult for him but at the same time to be clear that she and his father will not get back together again. She decided to ask Matthew's father to come with her to counselling to try to work out better caring arrangements and parenting strategies. She wants to arrange a more predictable contact schedule for Matthew. She also decided to see her new partner more without Matthew's presence. She hopes this might allow Matthew to settle and enjoy the time that he does spend with her and her new partner.

The long-term outlook for children

We have seen that we can expect some disruption of children's behaviour in the initial aftermath of separation. But how does divorce and separation affect them over the years? There is much debate about the ultimate impact on children of separation. The picture is complex and the evidence somewhat mixed—but the basic news appears to be good.

A review of more than 200 studies on the effect of divorce on children in Britain (the Rowntree Report)[12] concluded that only a minority of children are adversely affected by divorce. While this may still be too many for our liking, it is a very different picture from the one we so often read about in the popular press.

The Rowntree Foundation report found that the children of

divorce are roughly twice as likely to experience poor outcomes as children whose parents stay together.[13] This sounds like bad news. The 'bad effects' we are talking about include declining school performance, behavioural problems, leaving home at a young age, a tendency to physical illness and continual health problems and a susceptibility to depression or addiction. However, the basic message of the Report is that only a *minority* of children in both intact and separated families develop long-term problems. The only difference between the family types is that in separated families the minority is somewhat larger.

A more recent American study, which tracked 2500 people in 1400 families from childhood, reaches similar conclusions.[14] The researchers say that four out of five children from divorced families cope well. Within two years of the separation, the vast majority are functioning reasonably well. The report concludes that about 20 per cent of children from divorced families suffer some sort of serious emotional or social problem, compared with 10 per cent in intact families. The children from separated parents who were troubled as adults came mostly from 'families in which conflict was frequent and authoritative parenting rare'.[15] We look at authoritative parenting in more detail later.

The Rowntree Report stresses that parents and professionals should realise that most children make a successful adjustment to parental separation. They should be aware of the 'factors that contribute to a better or worse outcome for these children, so that they do not see poor outcomes as inevitable consequences for their own children'.[16] Very wisely, the researchers recommend that parents should be given information about the successful adjustment of most children. We know that what parents believe about the impact of divorce on their children will influence how they behave towards them and what they expect from them. If both parents, or even one of them, believes that the impact on children can only be negative, it may set up a self-fulfilling prophecy—expecting the worst to happen may set in process things that make it happen!

In a later study, the same authors summarise the issue as follows: 'Undoubtedly, parental separation contributes a risk for children, but the evidence suggests it is not *the* major risk factor. Children are not necessarily harmed by family transitions, but neither are transitions benign risk-free events'.[17]

This summarises the issues very well. Separation is a transition that involves risks. Sensibly, most parents want to know what they can do to reduce those risks.

Some researchers now focus on protective factors as well as risk factors, which appear to reduce children's vulnerability to adverse outcomes. One researcher argues, 'Divorce per se does not determine a child's subsequent psychological functioning. It is the nature of the conflict between the parents, the nature of their conflict management, their on-going relationship and adjustment and the extent to which the child feels supported to engage in an ongoing, open relationship with each parent that together have the strongest and most far reaching consequences'.[18]

Take the following stories of Marcos, Eleanor and Jake.

Marcos, 14, is truanting from school and getting involved in some anti-social behaviour such as minor shoplifting and letting down car tyres. He has not been a problem until now and his parents are at a loss as to know how to handle the situation. They are concerned that he may be experimenting with drugs.

Eleanor, 15, is showing signs of depression. She has withdrawn from her friends and spends a lot of time alone in her room. She is preoccupied with her weight and shows signs of dangerous dieting behaviour. Her parents are extremely concerned. She has always been an easy child and until now there have been no discipline problems. Now she is sulky and does not want to participate in family activities.

Jake, 12, is performing badly at school and fights constantly with his siblings. His older brother is doing extremely well and his younger sister is also happy and well-adjusted. Jake has always been the difficult one—

he cried a lot as a baby, demanded attention and was aggressive towards other children. His school reports have always been below average on achievement and behaviour.

How easy is it to identify the child from the separated family? In fact, it could be any one of them. The problems could be temporary or, as in Jake's case, they could have been present for many years. They could be the result of many things:

- Problems moving into adolescence;
- Bullying at school;
- Stress from parental conflict irrespective of whether the parents are together or apart;
- Parents having difficulty with relinquishing control and being too over-protective;
- One or both parents being too uninvolved;
- The child experiencing peer pressure;
- Pressure to perform above their capacity at school;
- Any combination of the above, or a myriad other factors.

The issues are, what do the parents and children do about these problems? What might have been done to prevent them from occurring in the first place?

There is no simple relationship between separation and children's well-being. Instead, separation and divorce should be seen as a process whose impact stretches out over time, with many other factors contributing to how well children eventually adjust. These factors include:

- The functioning of the family pre-separation;
- How well parents cope with the separation;
- The presence or absence of continuing conflict between the parents;
- The amount and quality of contact with each parent;
- The number of new family situations a child lives in;

- The child's natural resilience;
- Social factors, such as poverty and diminished educational opportunities, which are a feature of the post-divorce landscape for many children.

Many parents are concerned about what happened in the past and believe that the die is cast. While we can't change past events, we can, to some extent, change the way we think about them. This in turn can make a difference in how these events influence our thoughts and feelings in the present, and indeed in how we may experience the future.

What influences children's adjustment?

As there are several factors that seem to influence the course of children's development, perhaps the question we should be asking is: What can parents do to promote emotional stability in their children, regardless of whether they live together or apart? Put like this, we can begin to tease out the factors that might affect children's development. We can then look at what steps parents can take to influence their children's adjustment to separation.

Persistent conflict between parents

Unquestionably, conflict is a major factor that affects children's development in a negative manner, whether parents live together or apart. Acrimonious conflict is consistently linked to difficulties in childhood and is a more reliable predictor of poor adjustment than either separation and divorce.[19]

Children from consistently high-conflict families are less likely to perform well at school and are more vulnerable to delinquency and aggression. They are more likely to have poor social skills and social relationships and see themselves in a negative light. A number of children in separated families come from families that were full of conflict before the separation, so it is not surprising that they display some of this behaviour. When separation does not stop the conflict or, in some cases, heralds the beginning of new conflict, it is understandable that this group of children may have persistent adjustment problems. Despite continued contact and a relationship with both parents, many children are continually caught in the middle between their parents and exposed to uncertainty about what will happen to them.

Caught in the middle

When parents continue to engage in conflict after separation, children are often enlisted in the battle. This creates conflicts of loyalty that appear to have a seriously deleterious effect on children's wellbeing. A child put in this position for any length of time is subject to extreme stress.[20] Although this situation does occur in families that live together, it is a major risk factor for children in families that live separately.

At first, when parents separate, most children fear that they have to take sides and some even come to believe it strongly. Part of positive parenting after separation is to disabuse them of this notion. However, many parents become caught up in a vicious cycle of blame of which the children become a part.

Parenting styles

Conflict is only one of the factors that influence the quality of the parent/child relationship. After separation, the type of relationship that is formed between the child and their main caring parent is important. If residence is shared—that is, the child or children spend a substantial amount of time with both parents—then the relationship with both parents will also be critical. Four styles of parenting—authoritative, permissive, authoritarian and disengaged/neglectful—have been studied to see how they affect the quality of this relationship. The authoritative style seems to promote more resilience in children and be more 'protective' of them, while 'permissive child rearing and to a much greater extent authoritarian or disengaged/neglectful child rearing makes children more vulnerable to risks and post-divorce stress'.[21]

Put simply, there are two main tasks to parenting. These are to provide a loving environment in which to nurture children's development and to help children learn how to behave and act in the world in an appropriate manner. The authoritative parent attends to both these aspects of parenting. He or she provides both love and affection and sets clear limits. The latter is achieved in a firm but kind way. Children feel secure in this type of relationship. They know there are limits to their behaviour but they also know they are cared for deeply. This type of parenting seems to promote the development of trust, self esteem and confidence in children.

On the other hand, children with permissive parents know they are cared for and loved but, because there are few limits to their behaviour, they may not learn self-control and reciprocity—that is, how to take others needs into account. Children with authoritarian parents learn that the world is a harsh and possibly dangerous place. Their parent/s focus on teaching discipline at the expense of love and caring, and the discipline itself may be harsh and unkind. Children parented in this way may have difficulty in forming trusting relationships. They learn little about negotiation and may relate to others in an aggressive and conflictual manner, as they learn to model their own behaviour on that of their parent's.

Finally, children who have a disengaged or neglectful parent feel very unwanted. They have no one there for them and frequently feel abandoned. Their parent is too focused on himself or herself to be able to parent adequately.

While children seem to thrive best with authoritative parenting, there are a number of factors that may make separated parents more vulnerable to practising the other types of parenting. Many parents are focused on dealing with their own issues during the initial separation. They are overwhelmed by the separation and unable to focus their energies on the children. For the most part, however, this is a temporary situation. But as we shall see in later chapters, some parents are overtaken by guilt and this may get in the way of authoritative parenting. The researchers who looked at the four styles of parenting found that 'the permissive style was often prompted by physical and emotional exhaustion or by guilt' while the authoritarian style was often a response whereby the parents are attempting 'to control the chaos of post-divorce life'.[22]

It is also clear that an active continuing relationship with the non-resident parent, usually the father, brings many positive benefits. With separation, many children suffer the 'loss' of a parent. In Australia resident parents report that about 30 per cent of children have contact with their other parent less than once a year, or never, after separation.[23] Children themselves say that loss of a parent is the most devastating aspect of a divorce. Those who live mainly with their mother talk about their feelings for their father and express a desire for more contact. When asked by researchers (and they are being asked more frequently), children express a strong desire to maintain a relationship with both parents.[24]

The *quality* of this contact seems to be more important than the frequency of contact. An interesting analysis of the research literature suggests that emotional closeness and 'active' parenting are crucial factors in parenting after separation, especially for non-resident fathers.[25] These relationship qualities contribute positively to children's well-being after separation. Active parenting involves providing support, encouragement and non-coercive control—for example, setting and enforcing rules, reinforcing positive self-esteem in children and giving them positive attention. Active parenting equals authoritative parenting.

This contrasts dramatically with the type of relationship that is encouraged by the usual contact arrangements that apply to many non-resident fathers. These arrangements, such as seeing the children every second weekend, foster a more recreational style of parenting. This type of parenting shares some aspects of permissive parenting. The non-resident parent, as a result of having so little time with his children and because he is removed from their everyday lives, inadvertently fosters a relationship that is free from any stress or conflict with his children. The relationship focuses more on what the children think of him rather than on how he can parent them. The parent can become a 'visitor' in his children's lives and feels increasingly irrelevant.

The increasing irrelevance of fathers in their children's lives, when they play this mainly visiting role, may eventually lead to fathers seeing less of their children and gradually withdrawing from their lives.

Poverty traps

Separation and divorce are often associated with reduced living standards. It is difficult to make one family income stretch to support two households. In Australia, the Divorce Transitions project[26] has shown that sole female parents are at greatest risk of economic disadvantage. Sometimes, the same effect is seen in single-parent families headed by males. Having less money in separated families is consistently linked with poorer educational progress and outcomes for children.[27]

Lone-parent families are the new poor. Research tells us that providing economic assistance to sole parents is one of the most effective ways of dealing with the adverse outcomes of separation and divorce for children.

Another way of dealing with poverty in lone-parent families is, of course, for the mother to work. Mothers' employment can be a key to reducing poverty risks—most recent social policy research suggests that it is the vital key.[28] But work raises a further dilemma for mothers, as employment for them may mean less time to spend with their children. This creates another risk for the children, especially if the job also produces stress and fatigue.

The parents' relationship

Most of us think about parenting as a matter of how parents relate to their children. We all know a vast amount about parenting, learnt in our own family, from books or watching others, from discussions with close friends or through parenting classes. This kind of parenting involves identifying, consciously or unconsciously, the important values, beliefs and behaviours that we want our children to learn and then setting about teaching them by enforcing appropriate rules and behaviours. But this is only part of the story. It is clear that the ongoing quality of the couple's relationship is pivotal to the quality of life of everyone involved in the family.[29] If the relationship is positive, not only are the partners happier but so too are the children. Parents are likely to relate more warmly to their children and children to feel more positively loved and cared for. This, in turn, impacts on children's sense of security and stability, influencing how well they perform at school and the quality of their peer relationships.

So, how the parents relate to each other is a very important part of parenting, not only for the model it provides to children but also for establishing a context in which children feel safe.

If this is the case for children whose families are still together, how applicable is it to children whose parents are living apart? It appears that there is a 'minimum optimum' arrangement, constituting a cooperative parenting arrangement that allows flow-on benefits to children. This 'minimum optimum' can best be described as a business-like arrangement[30] that involves parents committing to a continuing partnership when there is a task to perform (bringing up the children) for the mutual benefit of everyone involved. Establishing this type of relationship requires parents to separate out their intimate and parenting relationship. For the children, this results in positive and stable relationships with both parents. It frees them to get on with the business of growing up rather than worrying about their parents or the state of their parents' relationship.

To illustrate: many separated parents become caught up in battles with their former partner over issues of parenting—issues such as the time the children should be put to bed in the other parent's house or what they have to eat there. These are parenting issues. They are underwritten by values and assumptions about what adults think is good for children and what rules should be enforced. However, the battle for supremacy on these issues between parents constitutes a far greater risk to children than differences in household habits about bed-time and meals. The constant tension and conflict that children are exposed to as a result of these battles, together with the negative modelling of the relationship between their parents, can create loyalty dilemmas and an environment in which they may feel insecure.

New partner, new trouble

A potential flashpoint for cooperation between parents is when a new partner arrives on the scene. Parents who may have cooperated very well until then suddenly find the whole arrangement disintegrating. For some former partners, cooperation was compromised initially by one of the parents moving in with a new partner, either straight away or fairly soon after the separation.

There are several considerations when cooperation falters over a new partner. For some parents, their former partner moving in with a new partner finally signifies the death of their marriage or relationship. The appearance of a new partner kills off all hope that they may reunite, and the end of the marriage or relationship finally has to be mourned. It is sometimes easier to blame the new partner and take on a victim role than deal with these issues.

Even if we accept that our former partner will eventually form a new relationship, it is genuinely difficult to stand back and allow that new partner to play a role in our children's lives. Sometimes, concern about what is happening to our children when they are with their other parent is really anxiety-induced anger about a new person parenting our children and a fear that this new person might displace us in their affections.

Since the quality of the parent/child relationship is intimately connected with children's well-being, it is important to note that this relationship is affected not only by separation but potentially also by a new partner entering the children's lives. We saw earlier how a parent's non-acceptance of the other parent's new partner could trap children into conflict between their parents. It is a difficult step for many parents to allow the other parent's new partner to share their children's lives.

Children have their own views on this matter. Usually, children enter a stepfamily after a period spent in a single-parent household. During this time they will often have formed a very close relationship with the resident parent. A new partner entering the family means another period of adjustment and a further realignment of relationships. During this period, children often become more negative towards their resident parent and there may be difficulties in establishing a good relationship with a step-parent. Children often find that their relationship with a parent, more usually the mother, is affected by the new relationship. If this situation is not resolved with time and care, the fundamental parenting relationship may be put at risk.

In a large research study of divorced and separated men in England, fathers commented that their children's relationship with their mother's new partner was a continual cause of stress.[31] Not only did the children complain to their father, but fathers were also in a dilemma about whether to intervene and risk their already tenuous relationship with the children's mother, or stand back and let their children handle the situation by themselves.

It seems not only the parenting relationship can be put at risk in this situation, but also the partner relationship. In Australia, about 50 per cent of second marriages that involve children from previous relationships end in divorce. Putting together a new family can be difficult, especially in the first couple of years. Chapter 8 has more to say on this matter. Ultimately, however, there seems to be no substantial difference in outcomes between children in stepfamilies and children in single-parent families.[32] Despite the difficulties, stepfamilies can be made to work.

Multiple transitions

Some children experience multiple family transitions during the course of their growing up. Their parents may repartner more than once and they may live in several different family situations. Multiple transitions do appear to pose high risks for children.[33] When children from multiple-transition families talk about their experience, they say that they feel less close to their parents and that the relationship is less warm.[34] It is not clear why this is so, but it does seem that children from families where their main resident parent has a number of partners have a poorer relationship with that parent.

We know that the quality of the relationship with each parent, and most particularly with the parent with whom the child lives most (assuming there is one), is closely linked to long-term outcomes. One explanation is that, every time there is a transition into a new family type, children experience all over again the stresses that inevitably accompany such a transition. Although these problems may be resolved with time, the additive effect of the stresses may well take its toll. And if these stresses are not short-term but translate into ongoing difficulties, then children from multiple-transition families will encounter all the difficulties faced by children from separating families but on a much larger scale.

This is likely to be the case because, by definition, multiple transitions mean that families are unstable, forming and disbanding many times over. Children may be confronted by all or some of the following stresses several times over and for prolonged periods:

- loss of relationships with significant people such as a step-parent or step-siblings;
- increased conflict with the resident parent when a new step-parent enters the family;
- less attention from the resident parent because of preoccupation with a new relationship.

Each time there is a new transition, the complexity of the child's relationships with other significant people is increased. It seems that each transition may increase the child's exposure to risk.

It is clear that the initial experience of separation and divorce can be a very frightening and bewildering experience for children. How both parents respond to each other and their children individually can have a profound effect on how the children come through the experience, both in the initial stages and further down the track. It is also clear that most children do make a successful long-term adjustment.

We know many of the factors that promote adjustment and resilience in children. Most of them have to do with parents cooperating with each other, respecting their children's rights to have a relationship with both their parents and believing in the importance of maintaining a relationship with their children. This is why it is worthwhile for parents and children to experiment with different ways of designing their family after separation—how these relationships are organised has a large impact on how children cope with the transition.

In separated families, as in intact families, the quality of the relationship between parents matters. It could be the most important factor in post-separation parenting—if the minimum optimum parenting relationship can be established, many other things follow automatically. Children will not be caught up in divided loyalties and exposed to continuing conflict; they will be financially provided for within a mutually agreed framework by their parents, and they will continue to have a relationship with both parents. All these factors reduce the risks to children from their parents' separation.

Where to from here?

Only by working together can parents achieve these things. That is why maintaining a cooperative parenting relationship after separation matters. Children have little control over their lives and depend on their parents to create a context in which they can thrive. In Chapter 3 we explore some of the situations in which parents find themselves after separation and look at the impact of these situations on children and parents.

3

Parenting pathways following separation

When relationships end, people often experience intense feelings—failure, self-blame, loss, bitterness, despair, revenge, anger. These feelings may be coupled with a sense of relief. The intensity of their emotional reactions can catch people off guard. Even partners who initiate the separation, while still believing that it is the right decision to make in the circumstances, can be surprised at the intensity of their feelings. At this time parents are vulnerable to being ruled by their feelings and often feel out of control. A natural response is to try to regain control but frequently this attempt is misdirected into trying to control the actions of the former partner. This is often a response to fear but it may result in a battle that continues long after the separation is finalised.

The main issue here is not whether people have these feelings but whether they allow them to dictate their behaviour, and to what degree. The feelings experienced on separation are a natural response to a difficult life situation. Separation and divorce attract high ratings on the list of stressful life events. How separating couples handle their responses through the process of separation is one of the major factors in determining what pathways they head down. Their future and that of their children will be strongly influenced by these decisions.

There are essentially three fairly distinct pathways that people can take following separation. Various labels have been used to describe them, but all correspond fairly closely with each other. One researcher talks about 'no-contact', 'parallel' and 'communicative' pathways.[1] Another discusses the 'single parent', the 'conflicted parent' and the 'harmonious co-parent'.[2] A third speaks of the 'disengaged parent', the 'conflicted parent' and the 'cooperative co-parent'.[3]

It is important to understand that many couples move between these pathways over time as they come to terms with separation and rebuild their lives. The most common movement is from the parallel pathway to a communicative pathway, as old hurts are resolved. However, a point of tension often arises when a new couple relationship is formed by one or both parents. The parenting partnership may be disrupted and once again become conflicted or parallel.

The communicative, or cooperative, parenting pathway

A communicative or cooperative style of parenting after separation involves parents continuing to work together to nurture and care for their children. In this sense, it is more to do with the quality of family relationships after separation than it is to do with any one way of organising care arrangements. It can take many forms. Parents on this pathway realise that an important part of children's well being after separation is the preservation of relationships with as many members of the family as possible. This includes relationships with parents, siblings and other extended family members.

If we look at three separating couples practising cooperative parenting after separation, they may all have different arrangements—that is, their residence and contact arrangements, their parenting plans, and their child support arrangements, will differ (the terms *custody* and *access* have been replaced legally with the terms *residence* and *contact*). The majority of parents will have the children living more with one parent but spending good quality time with the other parent, while some parents will negotiate a half-time living arrangement. Some parents may have moved away from their children but will still maintain a high level of involvement. They will have thought through flexible ways of having a long distance relationship and they will put a large effort into ensuring it happens.

Some parents on this pathway are friendly with each other, while others are still angry and hurt. However, the latter parents are able to contain their anger and hurt. They will usually manage this by negotiating an arm's length relationship, which has a clear structure. They see their relationship as a business partnership in which they make clear agreements they will both honour. They acknowledge that although they are angry with the other parent, the preservation of the children's relationship with him or her must take priority over their feelings.

Although child support arrangements for children will also vary among cooperative parents, there is one common feature. Parents believe that these arrangements are fair, if not ideal, and can at least be lived with for the moment.

So what are the essential ingredients for parenting cooperatively after separation? A number of elements seem to figure consistently in this type of positive relationship:

1. An understanding that the relationship with the other parent is a crucial part of the relationship with the children.

2. A focus on the well-being of the children.
3. Being creative about contact and residence arrangements.
4. The ability to set aside anger and bitterness.
5. Taking one thing at a time.

We look at these in turn.

The parents' relationship

Parents who intend to parent cooperatively after separation realise they must develop a new relationship with their former partner. This relationship is one in which each acknowledges the other as a parent and recognises the positive benefits for the children of having a relationship with both parents. Each parent supports and respects the other's right to be a parent. They communicate clearly to their children that the other parent is still their parent and will always remain so, and that he or she loves them deeply. These parents are aware that ongoing conflict and legal battles distress children and that children's problematic behaviour can be a likely consequence of their parents' continuing battles. Such parents also realise that one parent withdrawing from the children's lives is a hollow victory for the other parent. This distresses children, and while the other parent is not physically part of the family, they remain psychologically and emotionally a part of their children's lives. The parent's absence in turn influences how the children respond to the remaining parent and how they face the challenges of growing up.

A focus on the children's well-being

We are all aware that sometimes our own interests and those of our children do not coincide. This is something most parents experience. For many separating parents, however, it seems to present an extra challenge because separation is a time that by definition involves a clash of adults and children's interests. Most children when asked would prefer their parents to stay together. However, as most parents know, this is not always possible or desirable. We do not always do what children want. The decision to separate ultimately has to be that of the parents. But given this, most parents want to separate in a way that has the best chance of promoting children's resilience and emotional stability.

When we focus on the well-being of children, we are referring to the whole process of separation and the ultimate outcomes for children. It can be taken for granted that at times during the separation process there will be occasions when children's concerns get somewhat lost—for example, we argue vehemently with the other parent over minor matters or put the other parent down in front of the children; we are too depressed to pay our children proper attention. This is inevitable, particularly during the initial stages of separation when parents are learning how to manage their emotions.

This being so, what does a focus on the well-being of children look like? Parents on this pathway are committed to:

- Ensuring that family relationships are maintained for children;
- Ensuring that children are provided for financially;
- Communicating with children about how they are coping with the process and providing support for them where necessary;
- Giving children a voice in the decision making about arrangements, where the children indicate that they want to be involved in this way.

While the process of focusing on the well-being of children may be bumpy, when arrangements are finally settled, parents and children will feel that these arrangements for the most part reflect the above principles.

A number of factors can get in the way of this focus. They include the following:

- Emotions—a major task at separation is for parents to 'let go' of their intimate relationship while at the same time maintaining or even building their parenting relationship. This can be confusing and emotionally difficult. Some parents are not ready to 'let go' of their intimate relationship and instead focus on trying to hold on to it. This makes it difficult to build a parenting relationship. Other parents find the situation so painful that they want to cut their ties completely. They find it difficult to see how they can build a parenting relationship without having an intimate relationship.

- Ideas about parenthood—being a parent is a core part of our identity as men and women. Separation can threaten this identity by making us evaluate ourselves in this role. Women, traditionally, have been allocated the greater share of the nurturing and caring role. They may think that cooperative parenting after separation means that they have to give up their share. There is some reality to this, as they do have to partly 'let go' of their children earlier than they expected. In concrete terms, 'letting go' means letting children spend time with their father by facilitating contact and cooperating about decisions that affect children. Many women find it emotionally traumatic when their children first spend time away from home with the father after separation. It is a situation of loss and they have to adjust their ideas of parenting. Similarly, before separation women may have made more of the day-to-day decisions about children. Now they have to share more of these. Many fathers have a similar emotional reaction in respect of other aspects of the parenting role. We say much more about both men and women's reactions in Chapters 5 and 6.

Being creative about contact and residence arrangements

One unfortunate consequence of the trend towards more cooperative parenting after separation is that many parents believe it is about each parent having equal time with the children. This belief shifts the focus of cooperative parenting after separation from the quality of the parent's relationship with their children and the quality of the relationship between the parents to a focus on fairness. The attention paid to 'mechanical equality' is often more to do with the needs of adults than the needs of children. Children sense this since many children at separation are acutely attuned to their parent's emotions.

If the decision to share children equally is made on the basis of 'fairness to parents', children may well pick up on their parent's anxieties about their relationship with them and the parent's anxieties about sharing the children fairly. They will sense the competition between their parents. This can lead them to believe that they have to look after their parents and make sure each gets equal time so neither will be put out. It is the modern version of being 'caught in the middle'. One UK study found that the children who are least happy in these types of arrangements are 'those who feel they cannot talk to their parents about the arrangements and who have no influence on how their time is parcelled out'.[4] As one might expect, there were also numerous problems for children moving between households where parents were very hostile towards each other.

However, where the decision is made to share children on the basis of the children's needs and where the parents are communicating well together, children will not feel these tensions. Typically, children in this type of care arrangement feel they can talk with their parents and they feel as though there is some leeway to vary the arrangements. They don't feel they have to look after their parent's feelings. Sometimes they seem to get a bit 'fed up' with swapping around, but they also seem to realise that everyone has to make trade-offs. The same UK study found that for many children moving between households was routine.[5]

For this type of shared residence situation to work well, parents have to take responsibility for making it work. Children's moving between houses involves enormous coordination and organisation. It relies on parents communicating effectively with each other and being prepared to devote time to the arrangement. Otherwise, the children's lives will be chaotic. Equal or near equal arrangements do work for many parents and children. Children, however, as they grow older often wish to vary the arrangement. As they become more focused on friends and other activities, equal time becomes more burdensome to them. Parents in this type of arrangement realise that children's needs change and that the care arrangements must reflect this.

> A good divorce does not require that parents share child-care responsibilities equally. It means that they share them clearly. Whatever living arrangements and division of responsibilities parents decide upon, they cooperate within those limits.[6]

Following this definition allows parents to create an arrangement that will work for their particular situation, taking into account parents' work schedules and their availability to look after children; children's views; living spaces; children's ages and their activities, interests and school workload; children's friendship groups and their geographic closeness to these groups, and of course, finance.

Setting aside anger and bitterness

Learning how to deal with negative emotions is one of the keys to cooperative parenting after separation. Occasionally, people have very little stake in their relationship or marriage and separation comes as a relief to both. The dissolution of the relationship is a 'quiet' process, with each partner becoming more and more distant. The relationship just seems to fade away. Rarely do we see these couples in counselling. The anger, or what there was of it, dissipated long ago.

For others, their stake in the relationship and the current family arrangement is enormous. The threat to it and, therefore, to their identity as a person is powerful and arouses overwhelming feelings. Many parents become preoccupied with the unfairness and injustice of what they believe their partner has done to them. This preoccupation becomes the basis for blaming the former partner for everything that goes wrong in their own and their children's lives from that time onwards.

One factor that distinguishes parents who cooperate after separation from those who do not is not so much the *amount* of anger they have, but how they handle it. Cooperative parents may feel just as angry as many non-cooperative parents, but they do not feel free to direct it at the children's other parent. They recognise that this action would be counterproductive and unlikely to resolve differences between them. They know this because they have already had some very destructive arguments with the former partner. As a result, they make a decision to do things differently. They identify possible situations with the other parent in which they think they might lose control and avoid those situations. They use other people to help them negotiate when they recognise that it is unlikely they can manage the situation themselves. They look behind their anger and identify feelings of loss and grief. This enables them to handle their negative feelings and not let them dictate their responses. We look at further strategies for handling anger in Chapter 7.

Some parents develop or even maintain a friendship following separation, but a cooperative parenting arrangement does not depend on friendship between the couple for its success. Many couples for whom the anger and hurt is still very raw are able to manage the arrangement by negotiating an agreement that gives them space from each other by minimising their interaction. Gradually, as pain and anger subside, some parents find that they are able to interact more with each other. This enables them to introduce more flexible arrangements into the situation as and when needed, either by them or their children.

Few parents involved in cooperative parenting find it easy, especially at the beginning. They may firmly believe that children should maintain a relationship with both parents but are often surprised at how difficult this can be to put into practice. Inevitably, disagreements will arise but cooperative parents try not to interpret them in personal terms, particularly not as personal deficits on the part of their former partner.

If they find this too difficult, they try to put their interpretation to one side and not allow it to influence the resolution of the argument. For the most part, disagreements are understood as inevitable. Both parents acknowledge that they will be confronting new and uncharted territory where they will have to redefine their roles and the way they relate to each other. This task may be made doubly difficult because they will have less financial resources to support their parenting. Cooperative parents are also aware that one or both of them may repartner in the future. Such a step may require delicate handling by both parents.

Taking one thing at a time

Another characteristic of people who seem to be able to make this type of parenting after separation work is their focus on solving present difficulties and leave the future ones till they happen. Some parents are so anxious and insecure about the future that they want everything tied down for however long it takes the children to grow up. Cooperative parents, however, seem to know that the needs of their children, and indeed their own needs, will change with time. Their agreements focus on the present.

Moreover, in more complex situations, trying to solve too many problems at once seems to lead to overload and threatens the viability of the relationship, which is necessarily precarious at the beginning. Reaching agreement on one issue and concentrating on making that agreement work seems to create a basis for other successful negotiations. This one-step-at-a-time approach builds trust and addresses many parents' fears about the other parent's actions. For instance, some parents concentrate on getting the children settled first. This means that they might delay dealing with financial matters until the parent who has left the house has found a place to live, and can have the children over to stay.

Jim and Sally are one type of communicative, or cooperative, parenting couple (see box):

Jim and Sally have been separated for four years and have two children aged 11 and 9. Their separation was a difficult experience for both of them, but they were determined to minimise the impact on the children as much as possible. Both have repartnered and, while they have experienced some difficulties introducing new partners into the situation, they are basically happy with how this is working. Jim realises that his job does not allow him to take an equal part in the daily care of the children, but he is committed to remaining an involved parent. Sally works as a teacher and is able to be home for the children after school and during the holidays. Jim pays his full child support obligation regularly.

For the last three years they have had an arrangement whereby the children spend every second weekend from Thursday evening until Monday morning with Jim. The children's school is the point of changeover. On alternate weeks, he picks them up one night and takes them out to dinner or cooks dinner at his home. He helps with their homework, attends parent/teacher evenings and, on the weekends that he is not working, attends his eldest son's sporting events. The children's birthdays and other special days are celebrated together. As a family, they discuss important issues about the children and support each other's parenting.

Jim and Sally do have some differences about parenting and, initially, they tried to persuade each other to change the aspects of their parenting that were causing disagreement. After a while, they realised this was only producing more problems, particularly when the children heard them argue. So they stopped arguing and accepted aspects of the other's parenting that they do not like.

Recently, Jim has been offered 12 months' work overseas. His new partner is pregnant and both she and Jim would like the children to come for part of the time. Sally's initial reaction was negative, but she was pleased that Jim had chosen to discuss the matter with her first rather than with the children. When she examined her feelings, she realised that her negativity was coming more from her own feelings than from any reasonable objection. She knew she would miss the children but she had no concerns that Jim would run away with the children and not bring them back.

This was the first time she would have to cope with such a long absence. However, she realised that it was an excellent opportunity for the children to experience living in another country, and that they were at the perfect age for it. Sally also recognised that this time would benefit her and her new partner. Since they have been together, they have had very little time to nurture their relationship. Sally decided to take a risk and let the children go with their father for five months. She realised there were creative opportunities for everyone by resolving matters in this way. She had the courage to face her own loneliness and 'let the children go'.

Jim and Sally's arrangement is based on cooperative parenting principles. It is a good example of solving new difficulties as they present themselves and thinking creatively about them. They support and respect the other's right to be a parent and they don't undermine the other's authority with the children. Their arrangement is working and it has a genuine flexibility—it has the capacity to change as the needs of the family members change. They put the well-being of their children first, although at times this has meant that Sally has had to put her own immediate interests second.

Maria and Tony had considerable difficulty establishing a cooperative parenting arrangement (see box):

Maria and Tony have been separated for two years. The separation was messy and the divorce is not yet finalised. Initially, there was a lot of conflict about contact and residence arrangements for the two children, aged 9 and 12. Maria blamed Tony for the break-up of their marriage. Tony had an affair and left the marriage, although he decided not to continue this relationship. He rented a flat and wanted to have the children to stay for half the week.

Maria was upset and distressed by this suggestion and allowed Tony only minimal contact with the children.

Everybody was very distressed by the separation, including the families of the couple. Both their parents were first-generation Italian immigrants and there had been no previous divorce in either family. Both sets of grandparents were close to the grandchildren and were very worried about them and their adult children.

Tony initially decided to fight for 'his rights' to see the children. He was a very involved parent and cared deeply about his children. However, as he learnt more about separation and divorce and the impact on children of continued fighting by their parents, he decided he did not want to cause his children any more distress. He settled for seeing them every second weekend and one evening a week. Maria had been the main caregiver, working part-time for most of the marriage. She was home for them after school, whereas he could only do that infrequently.

Tony decided to be meticulous about sticking to the arrangements and supporting Maria as a parent in front of the children. With time, Maria came to terms with the separation and her rage began to ease. She saw the good relationship Tony had with the children and how much the children loved their dad. She also began to see that he was supportive of her as a parent. She tentatively suggested that they could renegotiate contact but she was still not sure about half-time. Tony respected this and the arrangement has now changed to Friday evening to Sunday evening every second weekend and one evening a week on alternate weeks.

They consulted the children about this. The children do not want to spend half the time at their father's house, especially the eldest daughter. Tony and Maria are now negotiating with the children's wishes in mind. Their eldest daughter would like a different arrangement. She would prefer to see her father more during the week and less at weekends. She is entering her teens and has an active social life. Staying with her father two evenings a week and Tony's attendance occasionally at weekend sporting events would suit the older daughter fine.

Tony and Maria are now thinking about having different arrangements for each child. They have consulted a family counsellor to work out a plan and have agreed to start experimenting with different arrangements. They have also agreed to continue to consult the children.

Tony and Maria could have been heading for trouble but they pulled back from fighting over the children and, in this case, it was Tony who put his immediate interests second. As Maria came to terms with the separation, she began to trust Tony more and see that he did not want to take the children away from her. They were able to renegotiate an arrangement that was more workable for everyone. They began to think more creatively about how to address their common dilemmas, such as the children spending some separate time with each parent.

It is crucial to emphasise that parents who cooperate in this way do not 'get it right' all the time. There is no such thing as a perfect parent or a perfect cooperative relationship after separation. In fact, if parents were to believe they had to get it 100 per cent perfect, it is highly likely they would fail miserably at the task. Cooperative parenting is not easy, especially in the beginning. Separation and divorce are messy and it is inevitable that there will be times when parents' emotions get the better of them. In addition, cooperative parenting after separation is a way of working together that takes time to learn and is based on trust. Trust can take time either to establish or re-establish and there will always be setbacks—such as having a row in front of the children, or questioning the children about what is happening in the other house in an inappropriate manner, or not letting a child see the other parent.

The distinguishing factor between parents on the cooperative pathway and parents who are on other parenting pathways is that they will realise they made a mistake and will try to rectify it and/or apologise for it. Each parent will make allowances for some irrationality on the part of the other. They will try, as far as is humanly possible, to shield their children from conflict that is frightening and overwhelming.

Cooperative parenting guidelines

- Support your former partner's role as a parent. Let your children know that you think it is important they have a close relationship with him or her.
- Unless you have a friendship with your former partner, redefine your relationship as a business-like partnership in which there will be clear agreements.
- Settle problems that arise between you—keep children out of the middle, where possible.
- Treat the other parent as you would like to be treated yourself.
- Remember: It is unlikely that you or your former partner will be able to make significant changes to the way you behave—particularly the behaviour that you disliked in each other while you were together—during the stressful separation period.
- Take one thing at a time—don't let all the decisions overwhelm you. Recognise the common feelings of chaos and being overwhelmed.
- Make decisions on the basis of the children's needs, not on the basis of mechanical equality.
- Sort out workable arrangements between you and the children's other parent and let the children have a voice in deciding these arrangements if they want to—but in a way where their voices can be heard without threatening their love and loyalty for both their parents.
- Don't let anger override your parenting objectives.
- Ensure that financial arrangements are fairly negotiated and children's needs are well looked after.
- Don't set yourself up to expect perfection.

The parallel parenting pathway

On the parrallel parenting pathway, contact with the children is maintained by both parents but there is little communication between them, or they may argue a lot. Parents may be resigned to the situation or they may engage in outright or covert conflict, the latter being characterised more by what is not said and what is not done (e.g. late child support payments, late drop-offs or pick-ups, negative looks, lack of reasonable flexibility). Resentment and bitterness is frequently high, with the parents blaming each other for the difficulties. Some parents will actively try to engage their child's loyalties against the other parent. There may be problems about contact, with children refusing to visit the other parent, or one or both parents not keeping to the contact schedule.

Children may also misbehave, particularly after contact visits. Parents often explain children's difficulties in this situation as a reflection of the other parent's behaviour. There may be ongoing litigation. Children may have to develop separate strategies for relating to their two parents and try to avoid upsetting one parent by their relationship with the other. Children may frequently be used as go-betweens by their parents, or they may feel that they have to look after their parents, pushing them towards a pseudo-maturity far beyond their age.

Typically, on this parenting pathway, the children live with one parent, usually the mother, while the other parent has contact rights. Parallel parenting is sometimes carried out through a 50:50 parenting arrangement but this is hard to sustain when the parenting relationship is in difficulty. Parents need to able to communicate about children's needs, particularly when the children are small. If near-equal care of children is being exercised, and there is little or no communication, it can be very difficult. If there is a high degree of conflict between parents and the children feel they have to take sides, then children living in two households are exposed to a much higher dose of the factors that may affect their lives negatively. This is a high-risk situation for these children, because of their continued exposure to conflict.

Some parents do manage to care for their children with little communication between them. The children are usually older and each parent basically parents alone. Sometimes, children carry messages between the households. While this is a more benign form of parenting after separation as the children are exposed to less conflict, it also carries risks. As children get older and need more supervision in their teen years, it is harder to keep an eye on their activities. Most teenagers push the limits, but with no communication between households there is no way of coordinating parenting responses if needed.

The dynamics of negative interaction

Many parents at separation get involved in escalating negative interactions. Each parent's criticism or attack spurs the other on to criticise or attack even more vehemently. Some parents reframe each other's character or rewrite the history of the relationship so as to excuse their own behaviour and also to place blame on the other person. Most couples that are separating do this to some extent, but cooperative parents find ways of pulling out of it.

Some parents are overtaken by this blame and negativity, pulling in family, friends and even their children to support their preferred explanation of the separation. These parents may become obsessed with the other parent's behaviour and tell themselves that they have finally discovered his or her 'true colours'. All other explanations of their former partner's behaviour are rejected in favour of the one 'true' explanation. Of course, the other parent responds to this reframing of their character by redefining the character of the other parent. Accusations and counter-accusations permeate the relationship and each parent becomes fearful of the other parent's next move. Litigation may be started as a preemptive strike or through fear of what the other parent will try to do, especially if children are involved.

A number of factors contribute to these negative dynamics—how the decision to separate was made, fear, power and control issues. We look at each in turn, but we need to remember that in many situations a number of these factors will be operating.

Unconsidered decisions to separate

Some experts suggest it is the circumstances of the divorce that trigger continuing negative interactions. Some researchers talk about 'impulsive divorces', which they describe as 'undertaken without reflection or planning or any real consideration of the consequences'.[7] These may have been separations that occurred as the result of the discovery of an affair, or as a manoeuvre to punish the other partner. These separations tend to be unilateral and come as a surprise. The behaviour of one of the partners has been secretive and the other is outraged and feels betrayed.

This kind of separation tends to be disorderly and chaotic, with parents failing to plan how they will manage the consequences for the family.

Charles and Evelyn illustrate this kind of separation (see box).

Charles and Evelyn had been married for six years when they separated six months ago. They have two children, aged 4 and 5. Charles has been having an affair and has left Evelyn to live with Susie. Evelyn found out about the affair through a friend and she and Charles had a horrendous argument, at which point he moved out of the house. Although both of them had been unhappy in the relationship for some time, and they had alternated between arguing and avoiding each other, neither had mentioned separation.

Evelyn is very distressed by the situation and very angry with Charles. She feels that she now knows the reason for her unhappiness and why the relationship was not working. The reason is the affair. Her family and Charles's family are also furious with him and his mother and father have sided with Evelyn. They have told Charles they are concerned about not seeing their grandchildren, as they fear Evelyn may reject Charles's family as well. Their joint friends have also taken sides. Evelyn has told them all the details. In fact, she has rung Charles's workplace on numerous occasions to tell his boss what she thinks of Charles. Luckily, Charles's boss has been through a similar experience so he is taking it fairly calmly.

Evelyn has engaged a solicitor. She wants the children to live with her and have minimal contact with Charles. At the moment, the children see their father irregularly, although Charles wants to see them more. Evelyn puts off contact visits with excuses of sickness or other scheduled activities, and rarely allows Charles to talk to the children on the telephone. When they do, she interrupts the children in the middle of the conversation. Evelyn gets especially upset if the children have anything to do with Susie, Charles's new partner.

Last week there was a nasty incident. Charles came to collect the children, but Evelyn was not there. He found her at the park and took the children forcibly. Both children were upset and, with Evelyn screaming at him, he lost control for a moment and almost hit her. This frightened him and Evelyn. His solicitor is trying to get the hearing fast-tracked.

Charles did not intend to take the children away from Evelyn. He thought that, being so little, they needed consistency and their mother. He was quite willing for the children to remain mainly with Evelyn in the family home but he still wanted to have a relationship with them and play a role in their lives. He feels that he is being cut out completely and he is now going to fight harder to remain involved. The children, of course, are being affected. The younger one has resumed wetting the bed and the elder one is 'clingy' and gets ill frequently. Evelyn blames this on Charles.

The story of Charles and Evelyn is not unusual. But how long can it go on for? A possible scenario is that Evelyn will be given residence and Charles will have contact rights. But this legal solution may not solve very much. Evelyn will probably continue to resist contact, Charles may get angrier and angrier and there may be more scenes in front of the children. He may go back to court but this probably wouldn't help. If Charles gets any angrier, he is likely to end up hitting Evelyn, and this would put him in a very poor position morally and legally. This situation is not atypical. Even though there isn't a history of violence in the marriage, the separation is so out of control that it provides a context for violence to develop. Typically in these cases, the violence is not ongoing but it can be just as dangerous and can induce fear in women and children. Inevitably, the man, in this case Charles, becomes his own worst enemy. His anger and the scenes with the children may cause the children to feel scared. Eventually, Evelyn will take out an Apprehended Violence Order (AVO).

Alternatively, Charles and Evelyn might turn away from a parallel relationship and move towards a more cooperative one. This could come about in several ways. One of the children might be referred to a child counsellor for help. The parents might be referred to separation counselling or mediation, as a result of the constant legal battles. They might realise the effect their fighting is having on the children.

For them to move towards a more cooperative relationship, a number of things will need to happen. Evelyn will have to acknowledge that Charles does have a role in his children's lives and that, regardless of how she feels about him, her children are missing their father. Charles might expedite this by acknowledging that the way in which he left the marriage was hurtful and it did not provide a good context for their future parenting relationship. Evelyn will also need to look at her own contribution to the separation and not focus only on the affair. Charles might acknowledge that taking the children by force is not appropriate but equally Evelyn has to decide to stick to the contact schedule. Evelyn will need to support Charles's role as a father to his children, as she has already undermined it in many ways.

Finally, Charles could compromise and give the children more time to settle before including Susie, his new partner, in the relationship. Instead, he might try to sort things out with his parents and spend more time with the children at their place. This would demonstrate goodwill to Evelyn and might be the beginning of a more positive relationship. It would also help his parents to realise that taking sides may not be helpful.

Any one of these moves on the part of either Charles or Evelyn could be the beginnings of positive change, a move towards a more cooperative approach to parenting after separation and one in which they could begin to think more creatively about how to solve their parenting dilemmas.

The impact of women initiating separation

Separation is more likely to be a unilateral than a joint decision (and is more commonly initiated by women than men). The unilateral nature of the decision to separate has deep ramifications for some relationships. For some men, the separation often comes as a surprise. Women will say that they have talked consistently about their unhappiness with the relationship and have reached the stage where they believe change is no longer possible. The men are astonished, believing that the relationship is basically okay. They find it satisfying and are at a loss to understand their partner's dissatisfaction. When the woman takes action, some men see themselves as victims and pursue reparation or punishment.

Parents in this situation may continue more of the same pattern they experienced in their relationship, except that after separation they swap roles. During their relationship they moved in parallel, not being able to communicate or understand what the other wanted from the relationship. The female believes that she tried continually to communicate her concerns but her former partner either consistently did not notice or underestimated the difficulties. Before separation it is the female who is frustrated and angry, feeling that she is being denied an intimate relationship, while the male is reasonably content with his life. After separation, it is the male who becomes disgruntled and wants to reinvent the relationship.

The difficult challenge for separating parents in this situation is to turn a parallel relationship into a cooperative one on divorce.

Fear of losing out

Fear is a further factor that precipitates negative interaction, particularly if there is a major discrepancy of income or finances between the parents and/or inequities in their involvement with children during the marriage. Threats, caused by fear, are often made unthinkingly during separation. Threats engender a reaction in the other partner, and they act defensively out of their own fear. Many of these fears have a legitimate basis and are usually related to gender. Most women, for instance, are confronted with the issue of how they will provide for the children when their husband or partner leaves the house. His income may be the main source of household support and she may feel that she has to move quickly to secure payment from him. The timing of the initial child-support request, particularly if it is made by the Child Support Agency, can increase hostilities, although the request may be quite legitimate.

Many men fear losing their children and fathering role. This fear appears to have some real basis given the large proportion of non-resident fathers who lose or do not maintain contact with their children—though the reasons for this are complex and still far from clear. An unfortunate cycle can be set up at this point where a mother will use her power to stop the father seeing the children as a bargaining chip for money and a father will use his power to give or refuse money in much the same way. This creates the perfect context for the development of a spiralling vicious cycle.

The battle for control

Many parents become locked in a battle over who will control the separation. Sometimes, this battle is a continuation of the dynamics of the marital relationship, where the main issue between the former partners was who would control the relationship—who would win and who would lose. These parents are trapped by their inability to resolve their differences and have a long history of conflict and anger.

Former partners in this situation usually have intense feelings of dislike or even hatred for each other. This seduces them into believing that they have let go of their inimate relationship. But the opposite of love is not hate, it is indifference. On separation, each tries to control the other's actions, especially in relation to the children. Fights and arguments are very dramatic, with each parent responding to the actions of the other in a negative and counterproductive manner. One explanation for their negative behaviour is that they are still locked together as a couple and have not come to terms with their separation. They have not had an emotional divorce. The separation intensifies rather than resolves the conflict.

Not all parents who fight over control at separation have had longstanding negative and conflictive relationships. With some, the differences have been buried and surface only when one partner violates the norms of the relationship. This frequently occurs when one partner makes a major change in life, such as going to university, which destabilises the relationship and brings differences to the fore. The partner who is changing their own life becomes dissatisfied with the relationship and begins to seek change. This results in escalating arguments, which the couple are unable to resolve. To settle their differences they each believe they have to get the other partner to change. On separation, the battle over the differences continues with each blaming the other for their hurt and pain.

Sarah and Tom illustrate this situation (see box):

Sarah and Tom have been married for 16 years and have four children. Sarah has been unhappy for the last five years but feels trapped in the marriage. Tom does not seem to understand her unhappiness. Their marriage is a traditional one with Tom working full-time and Sarah taking up part-time work as the children became older. Although not involved in day-to-day child rearing, Tom cares deeply about the children. His job is precarious and he is worried about being made redundant. He has been preoccupied with this issue for the last couple of years and feels that Sarah ignores his concerns. Tom thinks that Sarah's problems are more to do with herself than with their marriage.

About six years ago Sarah went back to school. She passed her university entrance exams and began a part-time Arts degree. She has been taking antidepressants for a number of years. She received counselling at university and has gradually reduced her medication.

They have not fought much throughout their marriage but, during the last year, they have begun to fight much more. The children have become involved in these fights. Sarah now talks to the two oldest children about their father and his faults. Their third child, a boy aged 10, is having difficulties at school and has been caught shoplifting recently. The older children—a boy and a girl—are starting to date other kids and Sarah and Tom are arguing about what rules there should be. The youngest, an eight-year-old girl, seems happy enough. Even though fights are unusual in their marriage, Tom still does not see them as a sign that the marriage is in real difficulty. He sees Sarah's demands as unreasonable and persists with the idea that Sarah's depression is causing all the problems. Sarah feels ignored by Tom and is beginning to think about leaving the marriage.

One year later, Sarah and Tom have separated. There have been more major rows which, in one instance, ended up in pushing and shoving. The three younger children spend some time every weekend with their father. Tom is very depressed and feels that he has lost out completely. He is living in a small flat which makes having the children over difficult. His eldest daughter sees him occasionally and his elder son is becoming more reluctant to do so. The two youngest, however, are anxious to see their father.

Sarah and Tom are barely able to talk to each other. Changeover times are very difficult. Sarah rings the children when they are with Tom, and complains about the state of their clothes and behaviour on return. Tom constantly complains about the amount of child support he pays and does so in front of the children. Sarah discusses Tom's behaviour in front of the children. The youngest girl has become quite withdrawn and the boy is having more behavioural problems at school.

Tom blames Sarah for the separation. Sarah responds by saying what a terrible husband Tom was and how he was the cause of her depression. She feels relieved to be by herself and can see some light at the end of the tunnel. She is no longer depressed. They are trying to settle the division of assets, but are unable to compromise.

Sarah and Tom are still moving in parallel. Tom is depressed and blames Sarah for all their marriage problems, now and in the past. This is a different stance from when they were married, when he failed to recognise any relationship problems. Now he does, but believes Sarah caused them. He would like the marriage back, but on his terms. Sarah has to change. Sarah is no longer depressed but she blames Tom for the marriage problems and will not countenance going back. The separation has worked for her personally and she would just like to have Tom out of her life. She knows that this is not possible but she believes that he is the one who has to change.

Power imbalances

In some situations, there is a power imbalance. One parent (usually the woman) may find herself being pursued and harassed through the other parent's contact with the children. He continues to try to run her life, complains about the way she is bringing up the children, threatens further court proceedings if she does not comply and generally undermines her parenting with the children. He may even subtly encourage the children to misbehave with their mother by supporting their bad behaviour.

The father may also try to exercise control by sabotaging time schedules. He does not come on time to pick up the children, refuses to stick to schedules and may invade her space by coming into her home uninvited. He may be directly menacing or the threats may be subtle. A mother in this type of situation may feel powerless to change it. She often believes that the only way to handle it is to put up with things.

Marsha and John illustrate this power imbalance (see box):

Marsha and John were married for ten years and have been separated for three years. They have two children, Kylie, 8 and Pete, 7. The children live mainly with Marsha, but they see their father at least once a week and sometimes stay overnight. However, they never quite know if and when he will come. He tells Marsha that she was the one who wanted the divorce, so he is not going to give her much of a hand with the children. He pays little if any child support. Marsha thinks that he must not be reporting all the money he earns, as she knows that he earns a reasonable amount as a builder's labourer. She believes he gets cash in hand. John says he is not going to give her money to spend on herself. He wants bills for how the money is spent on the children. John undermines her parenting and her self-image in front of the children. He calls her fat, lazy and 'a stupid bitch' and says no other man would want her. John takes over her territory and will not leave if she asks. He says that she is trying to stop him seeing the children.

Marsha is frightened of John. She has tried to facilitate regular contact but he resists all her attempts. She has asked him to stop undermining her in front of the children but he just laughs. She would like to have another relationship, but she is frightened of what John might do. So she puts up with it and heaves a sigh of relief when he goes. She no longer attempts to get the proper child support. She feels depressed and powerless. She is beginning to understand that he is still trying to control her. It is more of the same, as her marriage was also like this. This makes her feel even more frustrated and depressed because she left the marriage to escape from this form of treatment. Marsha has always believed that the children should have a relationship with their father but she is finding this belief harder to sustain as her children get rowdier, and more disrespectful and disobedient. She feels it might just be easier if John were not around at all as she cannot see him changing his behaviour.

On the surface this seems like an intractable situation for Marsha and it may well be. We have one parent who wants to cooperate and the other doing his best to sabotage this cooperation. John is as much in control of their relationship now as he was when they were married. Marsha has to make a decision about whether she wants to stand up to John and set boundaries. This decision is difficult for her because she is very unsure of John's reactions and she is scared for herself and the children. She feels almost paralysed. Some of her friends have labelled John's behaviour abusive but Marsha does not agree because he has not physically hit her. However, he has threatened her on many occasions. Because she feels so helpless and powerless, and because all the indications suggest safety concerns, her decisions are best made with the assistance of a professional counsellor.

The no-contact pathway

When a family takes the no-contact pathway we find one parent who is parenting alone while the other has very little or no contact with their children. 'Very little' means less than once a year. Statistically, non-resident parents (mainly men) are more likely to be the ones who lose contact with the children. This is deeply troubling. If we remember that what children most fear at separation is loss of a parent, we find that nearly 30 per cent of children get to experience their worst fear.

Many fathers say they also feel traumatised by losing contact with their children. A number of research studies suggest that fathers who have no contact with their children regret the situation and actively want to re-establish links with them.[8, 9] This runs counter to stereotypes of men who do not see their children. Separated fathers are often painted as selfish and uncaring, thinking little about their children and their responsibilities to them. But it seems that the story is more complex and we still have much to learn about why this happens. Some of the following factors seem to play a part. As is the case in all our scenarios, although we concentrate on discussing one factor at a time, many factors are usually involved.

Continuous destructive conflict—one parent gives up

One study[10] which compared non-contact and contact fathers found that non-contact fathers feel resentful and bitter towards their former partner. There were many differences and conflicts over a range of issues including contact with a new partner, contact with grandparents and child-rearing issues such as discipline and schooling. Fathers with contact reported fewer differences and had much better relationships with their former partners. The non-contact fathers felt thwarted and powerless, with little capacity to influence their children's lives. The mothers, however, had a very different story.

We also know that some men make the decision to give up trying to see their children because they think that the continuing conflict is more distressing for the children than the father's complete withdrawal from their lives.[11] This is a very painful decision and one they tend to relive constantly. One of their greatest fears is that their children will grow up believing that their fathers have rejected them.

Janice and Terry had to face this situation (see box):

> Janice and Terry separated when their baby Jackie was 18 months old. As Jackie was so young, Terry did not ask for overnight contact but saw her instead on Saturday or Sunday. However, whenever he picked up Jackie, he and Janice would always end up fighting. This distressed Jackie, she would cry and he felt Janice blamed him for the fuss. Finally, they agreed that Janice would leave Jackie at a friend's place and Terry would pick her up and deliver her back there. However, on many occasions Janice did not drop her off and the friend was reluctant to get involved.

Each time Terry misses contact, Jackie finds it more difficult to recognise him and she is becoming reluctant to go with him. Terry knows that it is difficult to sustain a relationship with a little one when he sees her so infrequently, and on strange territory. He has tried to negotiate time with Jackie in their old marital home, but Janice will not hear of this.

Five months on and contact has become more and more rare. When it does happen, Jackie is very upset. She sees him as a stranger. Janice is in a new relationship and Jackie seems quite attached to Roger, Janice's new partner. Terry feels that Janice constantly obstructs contact and that Jackie is being affected by the situation. Janice feels that Terry is playing games and trying to make things difficult for her. He did not have much to do with Jackie when they lived together. She felt he was more interested in his mates, football and drinking, and this was one of the reasons for separating. She is concerned that Terry might drink when he has Jackie but she has not told him this as she knows this will start more arguments. She hopes he will just fade away.

Terry has gone back to court for contact and it was agreed that he would have one day a week, but this is not happening. He has the choice of returning to court or accepting the situation.

After trying for another six months, Terry finally makes the decision to stop trying. Jackie is nearly three. She does not regard him as her father and finds contact with him very worrying. Terry is overwhelmed by sadness. However, he continues to pay child support and he sends Jackie presents on special occasions. He hopes that, when Jackie is older, she will realise that these actions meant that he did care and that he did not abandon her.

Terry realised that, unless he had Janice's support as a parent, it was virtually impossible for him to maintain a relationship with his daughter. To build a relationship with a child so young required a constant, familiar contact routine in which Janice encouraged and supported Jackie in her contact with her father. When this did not happen, Jackie became less familiar with Terry. The constant fights frightened her and increased her anxiety about being with him. The decision to stop trying to see her was very difficult for him to make, but it may be the best for Jackie in the short term, particularly if Janice will not support his involvement over time. Continuing to pay child support voluntarily and send presents will signal to Jackie that he cares and may, over time, lay the foundation for a future relationship. It may also signal to Janice that Terry is taking his parenting responsibilities seriously. With time and the absence of arguing, she *may* also begin to see things differently.

Separation is the end of the family

A common story in the past was that separation meant the end of the family. As the story went, it was in everybody's best interests to make a clean break, especially if the separation had been marked by conflict.[12] It was thought that men (and it was always men in this scenario), by not seeing their children, made life easier for everyone. Maintaining contact was thought simply to continue the misery and havoc of the separation. It was better for the father to get on with his life and leave the mother and children to get on with theirs.

The influence of this story is now far less powerful, but clearly it is still operative for some fathers. When they separate, they show very little interest in their children. It is as though that family no longer exists. The father may make some initial effort to see his children, but frequently will not show up at the appointed time, leaving them feeling exceedingly disappointed. Children in this situation feel their father no longer cares for them. The mother may try to interest the father in maintaining the relationship with the children, but he interprets this as nagging. After a while the mother gives up her attempts and becomes resigned to the situation.

Stephen's story illustrates this behaviour (see box):

Stephen left Molly for Esther. Molly knew about the relationship, but hoped Stephen would eventually get tired of it. She was reluctant at first to let the children go to see Stephen, as she did not want them to have contact with his new partner. She wanted them to have time to get used to the situation. However, Stephen seemed so engrossed in his new relationship that he did not make much of an effort to see the children. The children felt very rejected, so that when Stephen did occasionally ask to see them, Molly let them go to his new house.

However, the children felt very uncomfortable at Esther's and Stephen's place. Sometimes they were alone with Esther while Stephen worked. When he was there, they thought he paid more attention to Esther. They felt they were in the way and that Esther really did not want them there. Esther found it especially difficult to cope with Stephen going over to Molly's to pick up the children.

A year after the separation, the children hardly ever hear from their father and he has missed their recent birthdays. Molly has not pursued child support, even though Stephen is paying her only a small amount. Now that the children are moving into their teens, she is finding it hard to manage on her income.

Stephen's behaviour is typical of some men who seem able to cut themselves off fairly quickly from their first family. It is as though there is no genuine understanding of how this behaviour is affecting the children and their mother. He is preoccupied with his own life. Children in this situation can feel very rejected. It is important for the parent who is caring for the children to acknowledge their feelings of rejection and to disabuse them of any notion that their father's lack of attention is their fault. Responsibility should be allocated firmly to the father. Children are very distressed when the promised contact visits do not happen. Unfortunately, many of them experience this quite frequently.

Drifting away

Much of the research suggests that many men start out with very good intentions and plan to see their children regularly. However, over time the relationship with their children slowly dwindles away. Several things contribute to the slow collapse of contact. It is the reality for most men that they are the non-resident parent. They do not have the children with them for the majority of the time. Being the non-resident parent is inherently difficult. It has been said that 'many fathers drift away from their children after divorce because they are deprived of the opportunity to be parents rather than visitors'.[13] The argument is that men, because of the nature of the role they are expected to adopt after separation, become increasingly marginal in their children's lives. Deprived of daily interaction with their children and sidelined in terms of decision making, it becomes too painful to maintain the relationship. Another possible explanation is that many men do not see the parenting relationship after separation as natural. Parenting for them is an ongoing, routine set of interactions, not something to be thought about and separated out from everyday life. The loss of this role may contribute to their drifting away.

This seems to make sense—to be a parent, we need to be able to take part in our child's everyday life and act as mentor, guide or disciplinarian as necessary. The more removed a father becomes from these roles and the more excluded he feels from his children's lives, the more painful he may find it. The fact that the children do not appear to need him contributes to his feelings of irrelevance. That irrelevance reinforces the traditional view that children do not need both parents after separation and makes withdrawal seem a rational option.

Other factors also contribute to fathers drifting away. Some are practical, with geography conspicuous among them. In one long-term study in the United States, researchers identified that fathers who lived more than 75 miles away from where their children lived visited less often than fathers who lived within this radius.[14] Reflecting on American experience, the researchers believe that 75 miles is a manageable day's journey. Any further could make regular contact increasingly impracticable.

In Australia, one major study showed that regular contact tended to occur when children and fathers lived near each other (typically within 50 kilometres).[15]

Appropriate housing, in particular having somewhere for children to stay overnight, can be another complicating factor. And whether or not the father forms a new relationship and is supporting other children also plays a part. Tensions between the new and old family, time pressures and earning enough money to support both, are difficult areas to negotiate. It seems that some men give up.

Adam found himself facing these problems when Karen left him (see box):

Adam did not initiate the separation and found it hard to understand Karen's decision to leave. As far as he was concerned, there was nothing wrong with their relationship. He found going for counselling unsatisfactory. He expected the counsellor to try to persuade Karen to stay in the marriage. Instead, he felt the counsellor had sided with her and they ended up discussing separation.

Karen had been unhappy with their relationship for some time and felt that she had tried repeatedly to tell Adam this. However, he either got angry or walked away. When he finally agreed to come to counselling, she felt that he did not participate and this was the last straw for her.

Adam reluctantly agreed to be the contact parent, having been advised that men rarely got residence. He felt very unsure about his capacity to manage. He is drinking heavily and having difficulties at work. He is very depressed and feels defeated. The separation has left both of them in difficult financial circumstances. He pays regular child support but the settlement left him only enough to buy a small flat at a considerable distance from his children.

Initially, he saw his children every second weekend, but as time went on his contact with them decreased and he has not seen his children for nearly two months. He finds it painful to see them. He feels lonelier after seeing them as he is reminded of what he has lost.

Domestic violence and other safety concerns

Domestic violence and child abuse are other important factors that contribute to couples moving down the no-contact pathway. Where the relationship has clearly been violent and there is a continuing risk of violence to mother and/or children, it is appropriate that there is no contact. Although, children miss out on a relationship with one parent, this relationship is already compromised as is the children's health and well-being. The same applies to situations where there has been child abuse.

In some cases where there has been violence, it can be appropriate for contact to be continued. Some mothers are clear that, even though there has been violence towards them, the children are not at risk and do indeed have a good relationship with their father.

Some fathers also resume contact after taking responsibility for their violence and addressing the concerns of their former partner and the children. There are several ways of doing this, including attendance at programs designed to help men stop being violent, combined with the use of supervised contact arrangements to help children feel safe.

Where violence has been a major feature of the relationship, however, it is difficult to overcome the consequences. The abused partner finds it hard to trust again and to believe there has been real change. The parent who has been violent needs to understand that re-establishing trust will take a long time and that it cannot be rushed or forced. It may never happen.

For families in this situation, though, things are often not so clear-cut. The picture may be clouded by allegations and counter-allegations. Sometimes, the violence occurs only once, on separation, while at other times it is ongoing harassment and intimidation. Many men are just not able to see that their behaviour is counterproductive and that both their former partner and the children are frightened.

Women report that they are concerned for their own and their children's safety. Men frequently feel that false or exaggerated allegations have been made against them and they are fighting to clear their name. Women argue that they are denying contact out of fear, and men feel their 'right' to see their children is being violated. Children are often fearful, but men may believe that this fear is being induced by the mother and is not related to their own behaviour.

Sometimes, it is difficult to know what is really happening and, for everyone concerned, living with these problems can be very distressing. It is important that professional assistance is sought and proper assessments made. In these instances, legal assistance and intervention is important.

Alison had to deal with threatening and violent tendencies in her marriage to Mike (see box):

Mike, father of John, 12 and Ben, 14, has not seen his children for 15 months. Despite returning to court many times, father–child contact is always difficult, ending in conflict with Alison. On three occasions since separation he has grabbed Alison and, on one occasion, knocked her over. This resulted in an Apprehended Violence Order (AVO) from the court. There had been physical violence early in their relationship but not during the six years before separation. Alison, however, had been fearful of Mike during the entire marriage and, although the early physical violence had stopped, she was always afraid of standing up to him and continues to feel as though she walks on eggshells.

Mike was the dominant partner in their marriage, very much in charge of finances and decision making. Alison always felt Mike was critical of her. She had always been submissive because standing up for herself made Mike very angry. She found this threatening. She sees his behaviour on separation as manipulative and frightening and, although she has an AVO, she still feels unprotected.

Mike does not see his behaviour on separation as abusive. He thinks it is a justifiable response to Alison's behaviour, which he perceives as an attempt to prevent him seeing his boys. Since the separation his relationship with the children has changed, as they have become even more fearful of him. Their fear is not entirely new—during the marriage he had on occasions belted them fairly hard. They dislike seeing their father and, as they have grown older, they have refused to see him on a number of occasions. He blames Alison for turning them against him. He feels angry but powerless to change the situation.

Alison has remarried and moved to another city a considerable distance away. Mike feels that his place as a father has been usurped. He has tried to arrange to see his children a number of times but it has never worked out. Travelling is also expensive. He feels frustrated with the legal system and has decided not to return to court. He has now given up trying to see his children but remains angry and upset, blaming Alison for the situation.

The boys have ambivalent feelings towards their father. They are fearful but they also miss him. They have not formed a good relationship with their mother's new partner. They have angry exchanges with him about rules and behaviour and the eldest boy is becoming difficult to handle. Their mother doesn't know how to deal with this.

Mike's and Alison's situation is typical of many relationships in which there has been violence. With his physical violence early in the relationship, Mike established a pattern of control where he did not have to hit Alison to make her comply. She did so out of fear and she remained scared throughout the relationship. Mike does not relate to Alison's fear and doesn't see his behaviour as controlling or violent. He sees it as a natural response to Alison's action of leaving him. Instead of looking at himself and his contribution to this situation, he blames others and is then mystified when they silently resist. For Alison, this is just 'more of the same'.

She left the marriage to escape the intimidation but finds that Mike's behaviour has, if anything, become more threatening. Her solution is to withdraw completely and try to remove him from her life. The children are confused and do not know how to respond. Although she is happy in her new relationship, the boys seem less than enthusiastic.

Moving between pathways

Couples frequently move between the three parenting pathways. More commonly, movement is from a parallel to a cooperative pathway as past emotions and hurts are dealt with and the spectre of the former relationship assumes less importance in each parent's life. It is important to remember that, once on a pathway, the direction is not predetermined and inevitable. Many factors can affect it.

For cooperative parents, new dangers lurk when one or both of them become involved in a new relationship. Problems may focus on the children's response to the a partner and the tendency is to see the new partner as the cause of the difficulties. Generally speaking, the introduction of a step-parent into a family is a time of disruption for everyone involved. The success of the new arrangement will depend on a number of considerations:

- The sensitivity and maturity of the step-parent, in relation to both care of the children and acceptance of the former couple's parenting relationship;
- The ability of both parents to make room for a new adult influence in their children's lives;

- The state of acceptance of the former partners over their own separation.

This issue of repartnering is discussed in more detail in Chapter 7.

Cooperative models of parenting clearly lead to better outcomes for children. Most parents want what is best for their children and, while this type of parenting may be more difficult in the beginning and may often feel as though it conflicts with the parents' own interests, ultimately it also seems to benefit parents, allowing them to put bitterness and resentment aside and to get on with their lives. Creative solutions involve risks and take courage, but experience shows that they often produce better results for children and adults than sticking to more traditional solutions that can lead down the parallel and no-contact pathways.

In the next three chapters, we take a closer look at factors that make it difficult for parents to adopt a cooperative parenting strategy.

We focus on three different ways in which modern western society has thought and talked about marriage, divorce and family relationships over the past hundred years or so and look at the implications of each of these models for partners trying to design creative parenting relationships after separation. (In what follows, the words 'story' and 'narrative' are used as well as 'model', but all have much the same meaning.) We see how the legacy of these three narratives lives on, and how former partners may need to challenge ideas from the past if they want to develop a parenting relationship that functions effectively for them and their children in contemporary society.

4

What does marriage mean to us and how do cultural meanings affect how we behave towards our partners?

Listening to couples who are separating or even to those who come for counselling and are still together, it's hard to believe that the two people are talking about a relationship they shared. Each tells a different version of what happened—it is astonishing how two people who have lived with each other for so long can arrive at such varied understandings of the events that occurred.

Most separating couples account for the separation by concentrating on the personal deficits of the former partner. This has long been the favoured cultural explanation for 'failed' relationships. Couples seldom look at their relationship in the context of the society in which they live and what it is that society demands of them, both as members of a couple and as parents apart.

Cultural meanings about marriage and separation are rarely explored for their impact on relationships and we pay little attention to differences in a separating couple's perceptions of how their former relationship worked and what that relationship meant to them.

Yet those who dare to explore their relationship in the context of their culture find their understanding of their relationship enriched. If they are separating, it helps them to gain insight into how they reached this point. This knowledge may enable them to shift from a personal-deficit view of the world, which results in blame and paralysing guilt, to a focus on how the meanings that people attach to different personal behaviours create obstacles to building more positive relationships.

To understand how people will react to separation and divorce, it is helpful to know what they believe about marriage and the family. Their beliefs and attitudes are important in determining whether couples behave in a cooperative manner towards each other after separation. What did their marriage and their partner mean to them? What did they believe about how the marriage should be conducted and how, if at all, it should be terminated? What did they believe about parenthood and what values did they have about child-rearing?

Meanings about marriage, relationships, parenthood and family are grounded in our culture, from which we then fashion our own personal meanings. These meanings are translated into feelings and patterns of behaviour within our relationships and these, in turn, are important in shaping the broad pattern of our relationships with other people.

It is possible to think about such meanings as *stories* or *narratives* of what makes a proper marriage or relationship. We judge the appropriateness of our own actions and those of others by how well they match the stories we have in our head. In particular, we judge the nature of our relationships by how well they fit in with preconceived narratives of how such relationships are meant to be. Thus, in order to understand what is going on in a marriage, or what is going wrong with it, we need to understand the meanings the partners themselves attach to marriage.

Often, when partners come to understand that their disagreements and problems stem from these different understandings about relationships and marriage this provides them with a new way of thinking about their difficulties. It is a way that has the huge advantage of separating the problem (of confused or differing meanings) from the people involved in the relationship. It avoids the culture of blame. A form of therapy and counselling practice called 'narrative therapy' is built around these ideas. It suggests that those with marital and separation problems should seek to understand the meanings they attach to their relationship rather than blaming their partner for acting in ways that conflict with those meanings.

Over the past 150 years massive social change has occurred and with it has come a no lesser shift in the cultural meanings we attach to marriage, separation and divorce. Where once these meanings were settled and widely shared, there is now a wide range of conflicting views about what marriage is all about. Most of us don't associate these wider social and cultural changes with the problems we experience at a personal level. This is because we tend to believe that our partner shares the same meanings. Instead, we understand our problems mainly in terms of the personal deficits or psychological inadequacies of either our partner or ourselves. Putting what is happening to us into a context of confused, conflicting and ever changing cultural meanings often makes it possible to find solutions that are more innovative, more creative, more ultimately rewarding for our children and less personally painful than the solutions offered by personal-deficit understandings of the world.

In this chapter, we examine three cultural stories about marriage, relationships, separation, divorce, children and the family that coexist in modern western societies. In Chapters 5 and 6 we look at how these stories translate into relationship patterns both before and after separation, and how they interfere with the development of a creative parenting relationship after separation.

We learn most of our ways of behaving and thinking from the culture we grow up in. These values and ways of behaving are transmitted to us as children by our family and other significant people around us. Schools and religious affiliations also play an important role in forming our attitudes. Society makes laws that restrict the way we behave towards each other—we are not supposed to steal or kill each other, for example.

These cultural attitudes and beliefs change over time. Modern couples may live together in a stable and committed relationship without going through the formality of marriage. But changes like these occur at different rates in different groups in society, and there may be large gaps between the personal beliefs of individuals, or between groups and institutions like the church. Conflict can arise because we think differently from each other.

As we grow into adults we may change our values and attitudes, but changing the behaviours and feelings associated with them is more difficult. Our beliefs and attitudes contain elements of different and sometimes conflicting stories, leading to behaviour that is confusing to others and sometimes to ourselves. For example when modern couples decide to live together, they tell themselves and others that they do not need marriage to have a happy, committed relationship. While this remains the case for many couples, others find that they feel increasingly uncomfortable and insecure in the relationship. While at a rational level they tell themselves they should not need marriage, at an emotional level, marriage signifies for them a greater level of commitment and security.

The story of Bill and Lilly illustrates such ambiguities at work (see box):

Bill, 36, and Lilly, 34, have been married for ten years. Both have careers and both want a more egalitarian style of relationship in which they share roles. They have a five-year-old son and a three-year-old daughter. Recently, they have been arguing over child care and housework. Lilly thinks Bill is not doing his share. Bill thinks that Lilly demands too much. They find this conflict difficult to understand as they initially agreed when they decided to live together that they would share these tasks. Bill sees himself as a modern father and husband, and Lilly, sees herself as having a life outside of the family. Neither has ever imagined separating before but recently both have been thinking about it.

Both Bill and Lilly were brought up in traditional families, where the father was the breadwinner and the mother did most of the caring and home-making. Both sets of parents, however, were competent in other roles, with the fathers taking on some of the caring tasks and the mothers carving out minor careers when the children were older. Both sets of parents are still together. Lilly and Bill met at university and consciously decided to build a different type of relationship, one in which roles would not be so narrowly defined and in which both could pursue their careers. The conflict in their relationship intensified when their second child was born.

Lilly and Bill are in personal conflict, caused perhaps by having taken on new attitudes and values that have not yet been translated into behaviour. Both experience contradictory feelings and blame the other for the difficulties. Bill is surprised to find how desperately he resents not being able to put the amount of time into his career that he feels is necessary to advance it, and he is also surprised at how difficult and unrewarding he finds looking after small children. He feels socially isolated from his mates, who are in more traditional relationships. At the same time, he is having difficulty accepting that he feels this way. The fact that he and Lilly have different standards about child care and housework also creates complications.

Lilly finds herself in a different type of conflict over her roles as mother and career person, by which she is also surprised. She feels guilty about not spending enough time with the children and, when she does spend time, finds that she is not enjoying it as much as she feels she should. Her work does not provide as much satisfaction as she originally envisaged. She feels connected to female friends who are experiencing the same difficulties, but disconnected from her old female friends who do not have children. She has high standards about the children's physical care and care of the house, and finds it difficult to cope with Bill's more relaxed standards. Both regret the lack of time they spend with each other and the loss of their previous positive relationship.

Neither Bill nor Lilly has realised that, over and above their own personal conflicts about working and having children, there is a further dimension. To some extent, they are pioneers. There are no generally accepted maps to show them how to organise this new type of relationship and, although our culture now encourages more diversity of role sharing and equality in relationships, our institutions do not yet properly support this type of family. Neither Bill nor Lilly is employed in a family-friendly workplace and neither has the opportunity to opt out for a period of time to care for small children without jeopardising their career and financial situation. They don't have extended family support, as they have moved to another city for their work. To some extent, both subscribe to new cultural stories that suggest that a career and achievement in that career should be given priority over family and relationships. We could say that they are doing the best they can under the circumstances, but their relationship could be the casualty.

The story of Bill and Lilly illustrates the personal and interpersonal conflicts and confused signals that can arise from having two different stories operating at the same time. It also shows the magnitude of the impact of social structures and social policies on families. Having an extended family or a family-friendly workplace would probably have made a big difference to their relationship. When Bill and Lilly examined their attitudes and beliefs, acknowledged their ambiguous feelings and behaviour and looked at the social stresses on their relationship, they began to stop blaming each other. They realised that they would have to make some personal changes, as well as changing their lifestyle, at least temporarily. They began to attach a different meaning to their difficulties, and this produced new solutions. But, to do this, they had to understand the different stories about relationships that were operating in their marriage. They needed to look at the impact of these stories on their behaviour and feelings and the stresses imposed by the cultural lag.

But what if Bill and Lilly had not been able to take stock? What if they had continued to build up more and more resentment, blaming each other and fighting over how their relationship would be conducted? In all likelihood they would have blamed each other for the failure of their relationship. Each would have given a different account of their marriage. Whether they would have been able to sustain a parenting relationship if they had separated would have depended not only on how much they were able to set these accounts aside, but also on the cultural meanings they attached to separation and divorce.

Stories about modern marriage

Many young couples relate to the story of Bill and Lilly immediately because they identify with the dilemmas inherent in trying to build a more egalitarian relationship. In what follows we examine three cultural accounts of marriage and separation, children and families that coexist in contemporary society. These accounts relate mainly to modern western societies. Other cultures have different stories. However, as Australia is a multicultural society, many people are influenced by ideas about marriage and relationships from other cultures. Difficulties often arise with first-generation immigrant children who are influenced both by their family's cultural accounts and by those of their families' adopted country.

Our aim is to tease out the impact of these stories on our feelings and behaviour, particularly during separation. Each account of marriage has built-in assumptions about what should happen on separation and divorce. The stories also have implications for the way in which we believe a family should be structured and how we should relate to children. Understanding what we bring to separation from these stories can enable us to assign new meanings to our own and our partner's behaviour and open up the way to working more cooperatively.

Marriage has always involved two aspects: the private and the public. Both aspects have undergone major changes in the past century and a half. The public side of marriage involves the network of duties and obligations between men and women that are defined, structured and enforced legally by society, while the private aspects relate to the more intimate, interpersonal aspects of the relationship itself. In our culture, we usually expect to marry 'for love'. We believe that marriage will satisfy all our emotional and sexual needs and, nowadays, we also tend to expect that marriage will provide us with a context that will support our individual development and that of our partner.

The first two stories were dominant in western culture in their own time, offering an accepted set of 'truths' about how we should order our lives. The third story is now becoming the pre-eminent theme in contemporary legal and public policy discourse, but is more contested at the personal and relationship level. To the degree that these stories are widely accepted in a society, they provide common sets of expectations about proper behaviour relating to marriage, family life and separation. To the degree that these stories are contested, they produce confusions and conflicts that make conduct relating to marriage, family and separation more ambiguous and problematic.

The first story—Men and women: Different and not equal

This story was influential until the first decade of the twentieth century in 1914. It is based on the assumption that there are more differences between the genders than there are similarities. The superiority of men was ensured through legislation and men had almost absolute power over their wives and children. Gender differences were highlighted and similarities between the sexes minimised, with women defined as unequal and subordinate to men.[1] Roles in relationships were organised along strict gender lines. Men were the providers and women the carers. Men were the heads of households, women were financially dependent and, whether married or not, excluded from most public roles. Access to formal education beyond the most basic level was difficult for women, as it was for working class men. In many Western countries, women were still regarded as the property of men, first fathers and then husbands, with few legal rights.

The family was defined very broadly and operated within a network of reciprocal obligations among members. Child care and other family responsibilities, including the care of elderly relatives, were often shared among female members. Women's identity (how they evaluated themselves as people) was tied to their caring roles, while men's identity was tied to their roles as breadwinners and heads of households. Divorce was rare and granted only on grounds of adultery. For the middle and upper classes, custody and property issues were linked, with custody of children usually awarded to the father to ensure the line of inheritance. The allocation of fault was a central notion in divorce in the few instances where divorce occurred. Divorced women were socially disapproved of and excluded from middle class society. While divorce was rare, there is some evidence to suggest that separation was not. Denied access to easy divorce, people separated but remained legally tied together. For poorer people, this was the standard pattern. In these situations, de facto custody usually remained with the mother while the man was socially excluded or simply 'left town'. Remarriage was frequent due to higher death rates, particularly of women in childbirth. Family size was large.

Notions of childhood and the role of parenting were very different from the ideas of today. Childhood was shorter and children were expected to obey their parents without questioning or challenging their authority. Physical punishment was common and parents expected to mould their children's behaviour to ensure that they became proper members of society. In a largely conservative Christian society, children were seen as born into 'original sin'. As a result, they were inherently flawed and had to be taught proper behaviour. The emphasis in childhood was on 'moral conduct, conformity and fulfilment of moral obligations, to be achieved through practices that stressed regularity and differences'.[2] It was the responsibility of parents to inculcate behaviour that might ultimately lead to salvation.

Although both men and women obviously hoped for and sometimes succeeded in having an intimate and fulfilling relationship in this kind of marriage, this narrative clearly privileges the public aspects of marriage. Marriage performed the functions of regulating sexuality (mainly female sexuality), reinforcing gender roles, the upbringing of children, the inheritance of property and the maintenance of wider family relationships. Although this story was culturally dominant during this period, there is historical evidence to suggest that it was, substantially, a middle and upper class narrative. In Australia, poorer women in both city and country had little choice but to combine family-care roles with paid or unpaid work. Whether taking in lodgers, working in a shop, taking in sewing or washing or looking after aspects of the farm, their work was central to their family's economic life. In working class and farm families, the family with a full-time homemaker is a twentieth-century phenomenon. Many marriages were de facto and some children illegitimate, with illegitimacy regarded as an inferior status legally and socially. However, gendered role division was also a feature of these relationships. Women remained responsible for the caring role within the family, even though they had to undertake paid work to make ends meet.

From this brief description of the traditional pattern of marriage and family, we can identify certain assumptions central to its operation. These assumptions are listed below:

- Rigidly prescribed gender roles exist in which men have the role of providing for and protecting the family and women have the job of caring for the home and family members.
- Marriage is regarded as a contract for life. Divorce is rare and based on notions of fault and blame. Happiness is not the ultimate aim of marriage.
- Men are legally superior to women. Women are the property of men.
- The extended family and the network of caring obligations within it are very important.
- Children are the property of their father and have no rights. Children should be seen and not heard.

This first narrative emphasises an inherently inflexible approach to resolving the issues common in marriage and divorce. Answers are rigidly prescribed with little room for experimenting with how to organise family relationships differently.

The second story—Men and women: Different but equal

By the end of World War I, we begin to see changes in both the public and private nature of marriage. A story emerges based on the idea that men and women are equal, but different. This marriage narrative has become idealised in our society and is still hugely influential in forming our ideas about what constitutes the proper way to organise marriage and family.

From this perspective, men and women are seen as complementing each other. While women have more legal rights and are finally defined as individuals in their own right, roles in marriage are still clearly set along gender lines (men as breadwinners, women as carers) and this is reinforced by the way many social institutions are structured. Women have more access to education and work but this access is still limited. Married women had to give up their jobs in the public service in Australia until the middle of the 1960s and women received less pay for the same work as men until the early 1970s.

Within this story, married women for the most part are financially dependent on their husbands. This is an inevitable consequence of the division of roles by gender. The husband is head of the household by virtue of being the only wage earner. The notion that a household has to have a head rather than two people jointly managing it is very strong. Private aspects of marriage are starting to take priority over public aspects. The nuclear family model (mother, father, children) with clear gender roles is extolled as not only the best way to bring up children, but also as the model that will best service intimate adult relationship needs. Wider kinship ties begin to assume less importance.

In this story, marriage is still concerned with regulating sexuality. Illegitimacy is frowned upon and many women are subtly (and not so subtly) coerced into having their illegitimate babies adopted. Divorce is permissible, but not socially sanctioned. It is difficult and expensive to obtain and closely linked to notions of fault and blame. When it does occur, it is mainly initiated by men.

Care and custody of children is normally awarded to women, as women are defined as the natural carers. However, if a woman is found to be at fault, she may lose custody—the idea of rewarding the innocent party with custody of children is a competing thread running through family law decisions. A researcher on socio-legal issues[3] refers to the thinking that links judgments concerning (usually sexual) morality with outcomes for children. Accompanying this is a cultural assumption that it may be better to make a clean break on divorce. The no-contact pathway was born of such assumptions. Mothers and children can get on with their lives by finding new husbands and fathers and men can get on with theirs by starting a new family.

At this extreme, divorce really did mean that it was all over. Separation not only meant the end of the marriage but also the end of the parenting relationship. This view was further reinforced by beliefs about the psychological needs of children. Children were thought to need a primary parent. The best interests of the child were increasingly tied to the development of a secure relationship between mother and child, particularly in the early years. This period was frequently referred to as the 'tender years' and such a perception privileged women over men in relation to the custody and care of young children.

From anecdotal information we know that many couples did separate during this period, but these separations are hard to track as they were not legalised by divorce. In Australia, we had the phenomenon of 'the deserted wife' who, to qualify for state benefits, was officially categorised as widowed or, to be more precise, a 'Class C widow'. The relatively small number of divorces reinforced the belief that the nuclear family was both the natural and the only way to organise family relationships. Other types of families, such as single-parent families and divorced families, were labelled deviant. Separated or divorced families were burdened with a further label—that of the 'broken home'. So, while it may have been unfortunate to lose a spouse through death, it was somehow irresponsible to have lost one through separation.

But how are children viewed in this story? For the most part they are seen as vulnerable and dependent, in need of protection and guidance from adults. They should be shielded from the harsh realities of adult life, as childhood is conceptualised as a time when children should be mainly carefree and happy. Mothers were seen as essential to children's well-being and were advised that they should be the primary carers or they might risk psychologically harming their child.[4] Adults do not take children's views seriously, as children are seen as incapable of having opinions. In separation and divorce, adults make decisions for them. For the most part, children are seen as empty vessels that need to be taught and guided to do the right thing.

Summarising the themes from this story, some meanings remain unchanged but others have been modified.

- There is still a rigid separation of roles by gender. The right and natural order of the world is for men to protect and provide for the family and women to care for its members.
- Men and women complement each other and are equal. Men are allowed to exercise power in the world of work and women in the world of the home, particularly child-rearing. Although this arrangement worked well for many couples, women were financially dependent and hence, more vulnerable than men when problems or conflict arose.
- The nuclear family of mum, dad and the children is the best and most natural way to bring up children.
- Children need their mother more than their father. In principle, women were awarded custody but this principle could be challenged, especially if the woman was found to be the guilty party.
- In many situations separation and divorce meant the end of the parenting relationship. It was widely assumed that it was better to make a clean break.
- Marriage is regarded as a strict contract. If it breaks down, there is a guilty and an innocent party. Beliefs about separation and divorce and the operation of the law structure a highly adversarial approach to separation.
- Children need to be protected from adult conflict. Hence, adults should make decisions for them. Children also need firm guidance and rules. They have to be taught how to behave.

Solutions to problems in separation are just as rigidly prescribed as in the first narrative, with little room for experimenting with new and different ways of designing separation relationships.

The third story—(a) The same and equal

The period from the 1960s onwards has been one of rapid social and cultural transformation. Cultural meanings about marriage and divorce, children and families have changed just as rapidly. The culturally dominant story now is based on assumptions of equality and the minimisation of differences between men and women. Women are defined as equal to men in law and there are fewer structural barriers to women's achievement outside the family. Relationship roles are more fluid and no longer solely defined by the strict role separation of women as carers and men as providers. Women now define their identity through achievements both inside and outside the family, but a man's identity is still tied to his achievement in the world of work. It remains less socially acceptable for men to participate in familial caring roles.

Sexual mores have also changed rapidly. People do not have to be married to have sex and it is no longer expected that, if people marry or cohabit, they will have children. Women are choosing to parent children by themselves. Living together is socially legitimate. Couples are choosing to have fewer children, resulting in a greater emotional investment in those they do have. Women have access to education and work, and theoretically are no longer financially dependent on their partners. However, women still earn proportionally less than men.

There is a much higher risk of divorce for couples marrying today and, practically speaking, two incomes are needed by most couples to support their family. Indeed, a culture that once rigidly confined women to the home now tends to emphasise women's inherent flexibility, compared with men. Accompanying this increasing flexibility in women's roles is a growing acceptance of diversity in relationships in general and other family forms. Homosexual relationships are more visible and accepted; homosexual couples establish families and are more open about bringing up their children.

The private aspects of relationships are more dominant than in the past. Marriage, or living together, is entered into for love and companionship and is expected to meet most, if not all, of the partners' intimate needs. For many couples, the relationship lasts only as long as it meets those needs. More and more people are choosing not to marry, with marriage rates falling in most Western nations. Permanence is not sought in every relationship but, if people do marry, most expect and hope that it will last. However, in Australia, more than 40 per cent of married people eventually divorce.

The change in the character of marriage and relationships between the second and third narratives can be seen to involve a shift from following a clear map as to how men and women should behave in relationships to a position where men and women are encouraged to create their own map and to be flexible in the roles they fashion for themselves. As the public and social functions of marriage are emphasised less and the private aspects more, men and women have to take more personal responsibility for shaping their own unique relationships and for making them work.

They are also taking more personal responsibility for handling their own separation and fashioning individually creative responses to the dilemmas separation presents. Taking more responsibility often means looking at how each person's behaviour contributed to the separation, since both are seen as the architects of their own relationship. This leads to more creative—or perhaps 'designer'—separations which have the capacity to better meet the needs of everyone involved, children, women and men.

Women initiate the majority of separations. They seem to be more dissatisfied with marriage than men. A number of factors may account for this. Despite the fact that they also work outside the home, many women say that their partners do not seem willing to share household and child-care tasks. In one long-term follow-up of 1400 families, the researchers[5] found much evidence to support women's feelings on this issue. When they began their study in the 1970s, only 30 per cent of their women participants worked full-time. By the 1990s more than 70 per cent of mothers with children worked either full-time or part-time. The average man's working contribution (to the household) went up from ten to 15 hours. They suggest it is still the case that men and women still pursue their traditional roles, except that women cope with paid work on top of their homemaking role.

It is possible that this lack of role sharing is contributing to a rising sense of resentment within marriage and a higher separation rate. In addition, there seems to be a difference between how men and women generally view their marriage. It seems that women are more attuned and more reactive to the quality of their relationships, while for men the simple fact of being married appears to bestow many benefits.[6] It well may be that men and women have different expectations of intimacy and, now that there is more emphasis on the private aspects of marriage, men are at a disadvantage. Of course, these generalisations do not apply to all men and women. Both within and between the genders there are considerable variations and, in some instances, men will be more attuned to intimacy than women. We are talking here about general patterns that are more likely to be found in one gender than the other.

Ideas about divorce in the Australian context have also changed dramatically. Legally, we no longer assign fault and blame. However, while the law may have changed, many people's first reaction is to look for blame and to identify the guilty party. The fact that ideas of fault and blame continue to be influential helps to explain the persistence of adversarial practices in divorce, even though legal determination of such matters is no longer required. In disputed cases, the care of children following separation is no longer automatically awarded to the mother. The involvement of both parents following separation is encouraged and based legally at least, on the principle of the rights of the child to a relationship with both parents, and the principle of parental responsibility. The change in terminology from 'custody' and 'access' to 'residence' and 'contact' has been designed to discourage notions of ownership of children by their parents.

Recent changes in the cultural meanings of marriage may be viewed as a shift in emphasis from the public to the private aspects of marriage and family relationships. However, this obscures the complexity of the situation. Although there is much less regulation of the traditional functions of marriage, there has been growth in the regulation of other aspects of marriage, cohabitation and the care of children. These include laws to protect women and children from domestic violence, and children from physical and sexual abuse, as well as the regulation of child-support payments through the Child Support Agency. More recently, there have been changes to the *Family Law Act* aimed at enforcing contact orders. The state has also extended its influence to include regulation of the same issues for cohabiting couples. Many governments are becoming involved in work/family issues through policies designed to get men and women to share the load of work in the home more equally, although many would suggest that these initiatives are inadequate and not really likely to make much of a difference.

This story sees a dramatic shift in the cultural meanings attached to marriage and the family:

- Relationship roles for both genders are more fluid. Men and women are defined as equal. Men are no longer automatically heads of households. In fact, many couples would say there is no head.
- Expectations of relationships and intimacy are high. If our expectations are not met, we feel free to leave the relationship or marriage. However, if married, most people still say that they want a permanent relationship and most couples still say they want children, even if they say it is not yet the right time.
- Couples take more personal responsibility for creating their own relationships and also for ending them. Relationships and marriage are less predictable. As a result, many couples search

for creative solutions to help establish their preferred style of relationship.
- Separation and divorce are more acceptable, less stigmatised and, legally at least, not based on notions of fault and blame. However, while legal structures have changed, many of the adversarial practices that developed with the allocation of fault and blame remain influential. Many couples experience separations that are conflictive and destructive. Some couples still adopt a rights-based approach to separation, ideas that are based in traditional notions of ownership of children.
- Care of children is not automatically seen to be the province of the mother. The role that a father plays in his children's lives is more valued and he is encouraged to remain involved as much as possible.
- Divorce and separation are not necessarily regarded as the end of the family. Instead, they are viewed as an opportunity to make a transition to a new way of relating which allows children to retain a good relationship with both parents.

The third story continued—(b) Making children's concerns and wishes visible

In the previous narratives it is interesting to note that children feature only as appendages to their parents. Parents make decisions for children and children have little say over how they are made or how they are put into operation. It is not until the early part of the 1990s that we begin to see a major shift in the way we think about children's roles and rights in the separation and divorce process. Australia's adoption of the United Nations Convention on the Rights of the Child and extensive changes to the *Family Law Act* in 1995 have elevated children to a more central role in the divorce process. This is now having a major impact on public policy. Because this shift is so significant, it can almost be classified as a separate narrative. For this reason, we discuss it as a sub-narrative in its own right.

In this history of changed cultural meanings around marriage and the family, it is possible to identify change in the status of women as one of the major factors influencing the changing nature of relationships. Women have moved from having few legal rights (being the property of men) to having full legal entitlements as individuals. Attitudes to children are now going through a similar change. Until the Middle Ages, children were not seen as distinct from adults. Gradually, they came to be defined as separate human beings, but different, in that they did not have full human rights. They were the property of their parents or the state. Now, in a new millennium, we are in a period of transition with the child defined, in law if not in practice, as a person enjoying full human rights. This transition is occurring on an international scale. The United Nations Convention on the Rights of the Child is an important symbol and policy instrument of this transformation.

As more countries become signatories to the Convention, laws are being modified to reflect these rights. In the area of family law, and hence with application to couples who are separating, the Convention emphasises children's rights to be involved in decision making about their future lives and their right to contact with both parents. Children are no longer viewed as the 'property' of their parents but are seen as people in their own right, fully entitled to participate in decision making about their future. This change has important consequences for all family members. Some children in particularly complex contested residence cases may now have their own representative. This can come as a surprise to some parents who still see their children as their property.

This third story suggests a new way of understanding children's participation in separation and divorce. Children are no longer seen as unfortunate victims in their parents' divorce, needing protection from adult decisions. Instead, they are defined as capable of influencing and wanting to influence decision making that affects their lives. Children in this story are regarded as being naturally resilient and able to deal with with transitions, particularly if they are given a say in the arrangements. In this type of arrangement, children are consulted, listened to and respected rather than excluded[7] and powerless in their parents' divorce.[8]

This shift to a more democratic style of parenting is a natural progression when viewed in the context of how we now understand childhood. Children in this narrative are viewed as being influenced by their environment, their biological inheritance and, most of all, by what their parents do to them. Children need both warmth and loving affection but they also need structure. We tend to accept now that harsh punishment, as in the first narrative, is counterproductive to children's positive growth, but so too is overprotection and limitless indulgence. There is also 'a greater recognition that parenting occurs in a social context, and that the community or state can either facilitate or impede parents in their task of raising the next generation'.[9] Finally, we are also moving on to an era in which we are much more accepting of diversity, in that we recognise 'children's individuality and the active role they play in their own development'.[10] It is not all one way—children influence parents, as well as parents influencing children.

A more democratic style of parenting, while encouraging firm limits, allows children to learn by negotiation and to have age appropriate control over their own lives. The older the child, the more they seem to expect to participate in decision making about their future and to have these views carry some weight.[11] Parents listening to children's views and taking them into account is an example of this democratic style of parenting. It is similar to the authoritative parenting style discussed in Chapter 2, which we saw helped children to cope with the stresses of separation and divorce.

In Western societies, at least, we are also concerned to produce children who are capable of being autonomous and independent but who are also emotionally intelligent and interpersonally skilled. As we have become more concerned about protecting children from abuse, we have emphasised both children's rights and parenting practices that give children some control over their environment. We know that child abuse practices are rife in situations where children are kept powerless and without a voice both within and outside the family.

The dominant themes emerging from this narrative are:

- *Maintaining children's relationships with both parents after separation.* Children say that this is what they want and the research also demonstrates that, for the most part, this is what is in their best interests.
- *Fashioning post-separation parental relationships that work for everyone.* This involves parents being creative in designing their post-separation parenting agreements (see Chapter 7) and taking children's views into account.
- *Children's natural resilience* and their ability to cope with separation and divorce, particularly if family relationships are preserved. It is the quality of the relationships that matters most, not the structure of the family.
- *Children's capacity to have an opinion.* Although children seem to want their parents to make the really big decisions, they would like to be consulted, listened to and taken seriously when it comes to decisions that affect their daily lives. They want to be kept informed.
- *Divorce that is negotiated between the couple* and in which both parties feel they have contributed to the decisions, in preference to a divorce where decisions are imposed legally and where one party is the winner and the other the loser.

When we compare the third narrative with the first and second narratives, we see a movement towards allowing men and women the freedom and encouragement to invent their own post-separation parenting relationships which find solutions that suit all family members.

Although the third narrative has successfully challenged many of the commonly held assumptions of the second narrative, it is still highly contested in many quarters of society. Recently, there has been something of a political and cultural resurgence of ideas associated with the second narrative. This resurgence appears to be particularly strong in the United States but there are strong echoes of it in Australia. In some states of America, a new form of marriage called Covenant Marriage has been introduced in which couples, at the time of their marriage, agree to observe a longer period of separation prior to divorce, to undergo counselling and to base any divorce on legal definitions of fault. The revival of second-narrative ideas also includes a return to more traditional explanations for divorce, based on personal deficits and individualism. Research on the outcomes of divorce for children has also been used to argue the case for privileging marriage over other types of relationships. The renewed salience of such ideas demonstrates continuing differences in society about the principles on which Australian family law should be based.

There is also some concern with the third narrative and its approach to children and other issues such as domestic violence. As is the case with many stories in the process of becoming culturally dominant, there is often little room for experiences that do not fit the basic premises of the narrative. There is concern from some quarters that children who are affected by domestic violence or other forms of abuse may not be protected because the child's right to have a relationship with both parents is given supremacy, regardless of whether that relationship is actually in the child's best interests. We know that, in situations of domestic violence or child abuse, it is often counterproductive to children's well-being for the relationship to continue.

The rights of children to be involved in decision making have also become a matter of debate. Two themes are prominent in the opposition to children's participation in decision making. One theme is concerned with the possibility that children's involvement will reduce parents' traditional authority. The second concerns the overburdening of children with decisions that could pose loyalty dilemmas. There is a fear that we may not be taking a balanced approach to this issue. The child's right to be consulted does not mean handing over all the power to make the decision. The key seems to be listening to and involving children while making it clear that they are not responsible for the decision making.

In the next two chapters we examine in more detail some of the consequences for individuals of these different narratives of marriage and divorce and the conflicts and confusions they produce.

5

'Misfit' relationships: Consequences for separation

We have seen that the third narrative still creates much debate and conflict in society. There are two obvious reasons for this. The first is that it marks a far more fundamental transition in ideas than the earlier change from the first to the second narrative. The idea that men and women should, to the greatest possible extent, share roles challenges all prior conceptions of the relationship between men and women. Similarly, the idea that we should give children a voice is an almost complete reversal of earlier notions of what constitutes childhood.

So one reason that individual ideas and behaviour sometimes conflict with newly defined cultural norms and laws is that the gap between them is often very large. We often try to 'square the circle' by pretending to ourselves that the differences are not that great. But as Bill and Lilly found, this works better in good times than in bad. When we are under stress, we often revert to old behaviours or find it difficult to maintain new ones. We have not had enough practice at the new way of doing things. We learn our most basic beliefs and behaviours in our original families, but most of us were bought up in families that saw men as heads of households and women as homemakers. What we believe has not had time to catch up with where we are. A second reason that the third narrative is yet to become as dominant as its predecessors is that it has not been around as long and its policy support mechanisms are weak. We do not have a strong social context that supports this new way of organising relationships.

In this chapter and the next, we examine some typical confusions and conflicts in relationships that result from this vast social change in ideas about how men, women and children should be. We look at these ideas through two lenses—the lens of gender and the lens of separation. In this chapter we discuss how ideas and beliefs about gender, in particular ideas about the traditional roles of men and women, and ideas about the innate differences between the sexes, can lead to problems in relationships. We argue that to understand the struggles of many couples at separation, it helps to understand how they understood what was happening in their relationship—their account of the reasons for the separation. These understandings influence how they relate to each other after separation and may have consequences for how they organise their parenting relationship. As we know, a crucial task in parenting after separation is to disentangle the intimate and parenting relationships.

Relationship fit

Relationships that are working well seem to be more about how the couple 'fit' together than any one 'right' way of organising them. Traditional relationships—in which the roles and responsibilities are divided more along gender lines—and egalitarian relationships—in which roles and responsibilities are organised in a fashion that takes less account of gender—both flourish when the couple freely negotiate this type of relationship or they both have the same expectations about how their relationship should be organised. Successful relationships seem to be more about how valued each person feels by the other and how much each person values their own and their partner's contribution. They also seem to be about flexibility and each partner having the capacity to stand in the other's shoes. In this sense they are balanced, with each person feeling that they are valued and contributing equally no matter what form that contribution takes—that is, in either a traditional or a non-traditional way. This seems to create a context for intimacy, trust and respect, which in turn reinforces feelings of being valued.

'Misfit' relationships

'Misfit' relationships are those where partners seem to differ significantly in what they either want from each other or how they go about getting what they want. Some partners differ in how they want their relationship to be organised in terms of roles and responsibilities, others differ in their beliefs about what constitutes intimacy and how this should be achieved. What 'misfit' relationships often have in common is that both partners believe that their way of being in a relationship is the 'right' one. The result of this is that partners often expend a lot of energy trying to change each other, or one partner takes on the change role while the other partner resists. Sometimes one of the partners is so sure that their way of being in a relationship is 'right' that they make sure the other partner is not able to resist. In such instances, we have an abuse of power. In what follows, we discuss various types of 'misfit' relationships that are commonly seen in relationship counselling. We locate many of the issues in the context of our three narratives and we examine each relationship for the specific issues at separation and the impact upon cooperative parenting.

'Lopsided' relationships

One way in which relationships get into trouble is when one or both of the partners feel that they are contributing much more than the other and that this contribution is not recognised. We can think about these type of relationships as being 'lopsided'. Contributions to a relationship involve actions such as looking after the emotional side of the relationship, caring for children and other family members, keeping family friendships going, doing the housework and earning the money. Contributions are all the actions and behaviours that keep a relationship and family working and leave us feeling good about each other.

It can often be difficult to work out what is happening in relationships where one or both partners feel they are contributing more than their fair share. Much of how a couple feel about their relationship has to do with perception. How they perceive what is happening in their relationship now may or may not be connected with what is actually happening in it now. Past issues might be getting in the way or have so overtaken the relationship, that partners do not react to each other as they are now, but to some idea they have built up of each other over time.

But perception is all-important. It is what each partner bases their response to the other on. Some couples spend hours arguing over 'whose turn it is to do what', keeping a running scorecard. Sometimes one of the partners feels that they are forever asking the other to help but there is little or no response. The other partner may feel as though they are constantly being 'nagged'. It is often the case that one partner is contributing a lot more than the other in a specific area and they want to change this. Sometimes the issue is not the amount that one partner is contributing but the lack of recognition of it. Often these couples are stuck between traditional and egalitarian ways of organising their relationship, or the model that once worked for them no longer works and they are struggling with how to organise their relationship differently. Here we look at some common scenarios and see that many of the troubles in relationships that are perceived as 'lopsided' involve contradictory beliefs about how relationships should be organised and are a result of our different expectations of men and women.

A struggling egalitarian couple

Some women continue to work after the birth of children but they find the stress of their jobs, organising child care, finding time to care for sick children and doing the necessary chores overtakes their relationship completely. They have no time to nurture their relationship and often find themselves arguing over whose turn it is to pick up the kids, take them to the dentist, do the washing up and so on. We all know the scenario. Both the mother and father feel overburdened—they both think the other is not pulling their weight. Bill and Lilly, the couple we looked at in Chapter 4, fall into this category. It is difficult to find time to sustain an intimate relationship, run a family with young children and continue to build a career. Their way of organising their relationship does not 'fit' their present circumstances.

Traditional couples in trouble

Many couples opt for a traditional division of responsibilities when children are young and this can work well for many years. But it can lead to trouble down the track because what we want in our lives changes with time. The decision to opt out of paid work, or reduce it considerably when children are young, is often made on the basis of returning to a career or the paid workforce when children require less intensive care. But there is a catch—once having opted out of the workforce or a career, it can be hard to get back in, or if you do get back in, it is often at a much lower level. This can lead to resentment with the partner who opted out feeling that they have had to make more of the sacrifices than their partner.

Moreover, even if a mother does return to the workforce, a pattern has been set in the relationship that may be hard to change. Couples adjust to each other over time and ways of organising tasks, such as who does the cooking, cleaning, servicing the car, or attending to the daily routine needs of children, can become entrenched and hard to change. Children may unknowingly resist the changes having become used to the mother's way of doing things and having identified her as the primary caregiver. They come to see her as the main person to turn to in the family.

This can lead to the mother feeling that she is carrying an unfair burden because she both works and is responsible for much of what happens in the home. She may feel that her attempts to re-balance the contributions go unheard. This can promote an increasing sense of dissatisfaction with the relationship. It is difficult to quarantine other parts of the relationship from her increasing sense of unfairness. She wants to change the terms of the relationship but her partner either resists or just does not understand what is happening. The female partner wants to shift to a more egalitarian model while the male wants to remain with, or feels there is no realistic alternative to, the traditional model.

Egalitarian couple moving towards a traditional model

There is also a further more insidious problem. Many couples have an egalitarian relationship before children come along. They become accustomed to this way of relating and associate it with a successful relationship. Partners feel as though their individual needs as people are being met and they are respected as individuals. There is some evidence to suggest that when couples that have previously had an egalitarian approach to their relationship shift into more traditional roles on the birth of children, they experience increased individual and marital stress.[1] They have to either change their ideas about what constitutes a successful relationship and/or they have to alter their perceptions about themselves as individuals.

For women to make a successful transition into a more traditional role, they must believe that their new role as a mother is just as valuable and significant as their career or their work. Many women believe this but that is not how it feels when they finally become a mother. Motherhood is not highly valued by our culture and women often feel marginalised and isolated. They can find themselves reviewing their original choices about how to care for children, in an attempt to re-establish their old sense of well-being. This can cause difficulties in their relationship. Many partners may also be confused about these role transitions.

There are several ways of accounting for these types of troubles in relationships, but if we look at things in the context of change over time, we see that while there has been major change in women's lives, there has been much less change in men's lives.[2] Women have gone from being mainly homemakers and mothers in the 1950s and 1960s to having a wide range of choices about how they will conduct their lives, particularly if they remain childless. On the other hand, it can be argued that for the most part, men are still expected to conform to the traditional roles: 'men must be: 1) married fathers; 2) providers for, and 3) protectors of their wives and children.'[3] There has not been a similar revolution in their lives. It is still less acceptable for men to deviate from the traditional ways.

This difficulty is componded by the lack of institutional support for egalitarian parenting. We have made many changes to reflect this new gender equality. We have allowed women access to education, work and careers and have changed many of our ways of operating our institutions to make sure this happens (i.e. equal opportunity laws). But this is only half the story. We haven't done much to help women, or for that matter men, combine their roles as parents and workers. We still don't have paid maternity leave in Australia (although the government is now thinking about introducing it); we still organise the workplace as if there were someone at home to look after the children, we provide some child care but it is expensive and often not very flexible and we still don't encourage men to share the care of children by giving them paternity leave or flexible hours. Men still earn more than women on the whole, making it a financially sensible choice for men to continue to work full-time. In other words, our institutions do not support more egalitarian ways of organising family life, and without this support, relationships get into difficulty.

It seems that within the family, life has changed little. The upshot of all of this is that it is women who are more dissatisfied with their relationships, explaining why it is women more than men who initiate separation. Despite the fact that ending a relationship or marriage often means strained financial circumstances, many women choose separation rather than stay in relationships that are perceived as unequal and unfair because they are coping with both work and care roles. Birth rates are falling dramatically as women choose to delay having children or not to have them at all, because they realise just how difficult it is to combine a family and a career or work, and because they know only all too well who is likely to have to make the major sacrifices when children are born.[4]

So what are the implications for separating parents? At separation, official policy now seeks to encourage parents to stay involved with parenting by emphasising the child's right to have a relationship with both parents and parenting responsibilities. But for many parents this requires a transition from traditional parenting roles in marriage or the relationship to more egalitarian parenting roles on separation. In more egalitarian-type relationships, there is already a context of shared parenting before separation, which can make the transition into shared parenting on separation easier. If Bill and Lilly were to separate, the fact that they have shared parenting in their relationship may allow them both to acknowledge the importance of remaining involved in this way.

In what follows, we identify beliefs and behaviours that are embedded in the types of relationships we have discussed so far. These factors can create major challenges for parents at separation and unless addressed may affect their capacity to parent cooperatively. While we address these factors separately, it is again often the case that a number of factors are at play, each simultaneously reinforcing each other.

Traditional fathering

There is much debate about the role of fathers in families but one line of argument suggests that traditional relationships predispose fathers to depend heavily on mothers to support their relationship with their children. Once a traditional division of labour is established in the family, the structure of these roles reinforces the mother as the 'hands-on' or primary parent. Fathers need mothers to keep them informed and often rely on them to tell them how to respond to the children and their day-to-day concerns.[5] In this sense, while fathers are members of a parental team, mothers take more responsibility for the actual parenting.[6]

Full-time work means that men spend less time with the children than their mother does. Children are therefore more likely to form their primary relationship with their mother, especially in the early years. Mothers also form a particular bond with their children through pregnancy and breastfeeding, and, of course, it is precisely in these early years that children learn that it is women who are the 'proper' providers of care and affection. One area of parenting where fathers have had more of a role is in disciplining children. But even here fathers rely heavily on mothers' communication about the behaviour of the children. This is typified in the northern English mother's song: 'Ee, thou art a mucky kid, dirty as a dustbin lid. When he hears the things you did, you'll get a belt from your daddy.'

According to this argument, on separation, fathers have to negotiate a new role with their children if they are going to remain involved and share parenting responsibilities with their former partner. The loss of his day-to-day involvement and the change in the mother's support for his role as a father make it difficult for him to continue to father in the traditional way. In Chapter 3, we suggested that a number of mutually reinforcing dynamics could lead to men becoming visitors in their children's lives. This parcelling together of marriage and fatherhood provides a context for these dynamics to thrive and illustrates the complexity of the issues involved in trying to make the transition from traditional parenting roles in a relationship to more egalitarian parenting roles at separation. Fathers and mother need to be aware of this vulnerability in designing their post-separation arrangements.

Women's identity as a mother

In traditional relationships and in 'misfit' relationships, where the mother feels that she has been the one who has carried the main parenting load, women may be more likely to define their role as mother as a core part of their identity. Separation threatens this identity. This can make it hard for her to agree to a co-parenting arrangement on separation. We discussed in Chapter 3 how many women have to come to terms with 'letting go' of their children early and how difficult this can be. It is further complicated by the fact that there may be genuine concerns about the other parent's capacity to care for the children as the father has not demonstrated that he can do so or wished to do so in the past. This can lead to resentment.

The role of resentment

In 'misfit' relationships, where the mother in particular feels she has been carrying an unfair load, she will often feel enormous resentment when the father becomes or wishes to become more involved in hands-on parenting at separation. From the mother's point of view, it is this very lack of active involvement that was the source of frustration and conflict in the relationship. She finds it hard to understand that it is her decision to separate that serves as the catalyst for the father's change. The separation makes him realise just how much he does care about his family and the need for change in his parenting role. Sometimes it is only when we lose something that we realise how much we value it. However, this realisation often comes when it is too late for the relationship as too much damage has been done to the structure of intimacy and trust which holds it together.

Many fathers reach this realisation after a long struggle with depression and guilt in which they reflect on their marriage or relationship. The change may be genuine but for mothers it is hard to accept that the person she is now relating to in separation is more like the person she wanted him to be when they were together. She may mistrust the change, thinking that he is either trying to punish her—by taking away her role—or trying to control her because he is making suggestions that she experiences as demands.

This type of resentment can play havoc with cooperative parenting at separation. Instead of focusing on their responsibilities as parents and the needs of the children, mothers who understandably feel this resentment allow it to overtake them and dictate their behaviour and decisions. They may fight to limit the father's involvement believing that he does not deserve to be more involved with the children since he was much less involved in a day-to-day way when they were together. This can be justified by saying he had the opportunity and he did not take it! We are looking here at second narrative solutions of fault and blame.

The creative response to this is for a mother to examine her own motives and think back to the times when she was happy in the realtionship. She should ask herself whether she would have thought it was okay for the children to grow up without a meaningful relationship with their father. She should also ask herself if she is allowing past hurts to rule her decisions about the future and reflect on whether her desire to push the other parent away is connected to her own sense of impending loss.

Helping the family make the transition

Fathers who genuinely wish to be more involved with their children after separation often find that some of the mother's objections and fears can be overcome if they slow down the negotiation process and acknowledge her genuine concerns and her resentment. They acknowledge that the relationship with the other parent has been one in which she did take more responsibility for the children and they acknowledge that while separation is a big transition for the family, his involvement with more active parenting is a further transition. This latter transition may well be more successful if taken slowly and an investment made in building trust and confidence. This means demonstrating that he is focused on the needs of the children. Supporting the mother in her parenting role, sorting out child support arrangements and demonstrating that he takes the role of looking after the day-to-day needs of children seriously, are all ways of doing this. When fathers take this approach to dealing with resentment fuelled by conflicts, they are acting from a principle of care[7] rather than from some abstract principle of what is just or fair.

Jen and Chris's situation illustrates parents caught in these types of dilemmas (see box):

Jen and Chris have lived together for ten years and have two children—Lisa, 7 and Luke, 6. Jen and Chris have both worked full-time for most of these years with Jen taking off a couple of months after the birth of each child. They managed to juggle work and home with the support of Jen's mother and child care. Things worked reasonably well until Jen's mother became ill and instead of Jen's mum helping with the children, Jen had to spend a lot of time supporting her mother and father. Chris has a good relationship with the children. He spends a lot of time playing with them and they like to help him around the house. He is important in their lives but they see their mother as the main one who looks after them.

Jen has become increasingly disaffected with their relationship over the past couple of years. She feels that she carries most of the load. This would not be so bad if she felt close to Chris but she feels very disconnected from him. Chris feels that Jen is always complaining and he resents the loss of their sexual relationship. He thinks if only they could get this working again that other things would get better. Every time he attempts to help Jen he feels criticised by her.

Since they have separated, Chris has been overwhelmed with anxiety and depression. From time to time, he has felt suicidal. When he has the children, he struggles to look after them. Jen was concerned for the children's welfare and they began to see less of their father. Chris finally went for counselling and started to come to terms with the separation. As his mental health improved and he started to understand how the relationship had unravelled, he wanted to spend more time with the children. He also felt more capable of looking after them, although he realised he had a lot to learn.

Jen found that she was feeling incensed at Chris wanting to spend more time with the children. She had never felt such rage before. She realised that much of the rage related to the fact that she felt the relationship had been very unfair. She even felt the separation had been unfair in that she had to cope with the children while Chris fell apart. She resisted his efforts to see more of the children. Eventually, they met for coffee one evening to discuss arrangements but the conversation developed into a slinging match and Jen left feeling angrier than ever. Chris felt miserable and uncertain about what to do.

Some days later Chris rang Jen and asked if she would go to child-focused mediation. He had seen his counsellor who had explored with him why Jen might be feeling so angry and he found he could understand this. He began to understand that he wanted to change the terms of the relationship and he realised that this was a momentous change for everyone to deal with. He explored with the counsellor whether this was really in the best interests of the children or whether it might be better to take things slowly and give the children a voice in the process.

Jen has been careful to be positive to the children about their father and they have talked to her about missing him. She struggled with her emotions but agreed to go to mediation because she really did care about the children and she knew how she felt was not really helpful to them or herself in the long term. The mediation was very stressful but very helpful. Both agreed to the children being involved. Their children saw a professional who fed back to them how the children were feeling and seeing the world. The children were concerned about both their parents. They missed their father and they sensed how sad he had been. However, they were also aware he was feeling much better and they did want to see him more.

Both children felt that they would like to sleep over at their father's but they were a bit confused about how that would work and what it would feel like. When they had stayed before, it had not worked too well because their father was depressed. Both of them also wanted him to come to their activities and be involved with some of their sports. Most of all, both children wanted their parents to sort things out. They sensed that there was trouble and this worried them.

Jen and Chris reached an initial agreement. The children would stay over one night a week to begin with and Chris would take them to some of their sporting activities on the weekend. Chris would pick them up from school and drop them back at school the next day. He would also take the kids to some of their activities on his rostered day off. They would review the situation in three months, at the mediation service.

Gender-specific attitudes

Differences in what is expected of men and women in roles within the family and the world of work are only aspects of a wider process of socialisation. Many of our basic assumptions about gender and relationships are learnt in our family of origin, with boys and girls being socialised very differently. This early socialisation forms the basis for our masculine and feminine identities, leading to distinct psychological profiles for men and women which cannot easily be overcome in only a few generations.[8,9] This has implications for a couple's expectations regarding intimacy in their relationship. It is particularly relevant when the success of relationships or marriages is based mainly on the individual's personal judgment about how much it fulfils his or her intimacy needs, which is the main criteria of judgment in the third narrative.

In a world where the third narrative progressively shapes and reshapes our institutions and our cultural expectations, our attitudes and behavioural assumptions still often conform to the second-narrative model we acquired in childhood. Although traditional forms of relationships can be stifling for both women and men, the expectations about male and female behaviour embodied in the newer narratives can also be 'crazy-making' because they deny the differences between the genders established as 'natural' since childhood.[10] This may result in confusions and tensions in relationships as men and women struggle to define new relationships for which there are few maps and for which they are still not psychologically equipped.

It is important, however, not to overemphasise these attitude differences. While there do seem to be identifiable patterns of attitudes and behaviour that are associated with one gender more than the other at a general level, there are still more differences within the genders than there are between them. This is clearly supported by relationship counselling work with gay couples. They present with many of the same issues as heterosexual couples.[11] Some of these are structural, such as the pressure of work on the relationship, especially if they are caring for children, while others are more individual, such as differences around what they personally want from their relationship. Gender is only one lens that may be used to understand relationships. There are many others and they all contribute to a much richer picture of relationships and marriage.

Common gender differences cluster around the notion that men are more instrumental or outcome-focused and women more relationship-oriented. Similarly, men are said to be more dominant and in control, with women less rational and more dependent. On the other hand, gender socialisation is becoming more fluid, with many boys and girls now receiving less stereotyped messages than was once the case. Problems arise with these types of gender messages when individuals are ambivalent about what they believe and when couples confront contradictory or ambivalent messages.

Bob and Susie had been having marital problems for some time. Susie complained about Bob's lack of communication and the lack of what she called intimacy in their relationship. She felt that she took all the responsibility for looking after the emotional side of the relationship and she wanted Bob to relate more warmly to her, to show his emotions and to be more affectionate and caring in the relationship. She wanted him to say what he really felt. She talked about separation if the situation did not improve. During one of the counselling sessions, Bob became quite upset and started to cry. He talked about the ways in which he did care for Susie and the fact that he felt that he would never measure up to what she wanted. Susie found the session more and more difficult and in fact became quite uncomfortable and somewhat angry. When we started to unpack her anger, it became clear that she felt very uncomfortable with Bob crying. She found the idea of men crying quite difficult and she saw Bob as weak for doing so. She also felt that he should not be concerned about measuring up to her. She felt that he should be the more dominant person in the relationship and she resented the fact that she saw him as the weaker person. This was a surprise to her. She felt cross with herself because she discovered that what she thought she wanted in a man was not what she really wanted at all. She thought she wanted a partner who could show his softer, more vulnerable side. Yet, when he did so, she became very uncomfortable. Bob sensed this and withdrew more.

There are many more examples of such confusions stemming from lags or ambivalences in our personal, relationship and cultural narratives. Sometimes men take on the protector role in relation to women and sometimes that is what women want. At other times, protection is the last thing women want and such behaviour incenses them. Neither men nor women seem to be able to work out what is the right time for the right response. Men are also said to be more action-oriented and women more relationship-oriented. It is part of being masculine to take control and try and solve the problem. Frequently, all women want is 'someone to listen to them', but men often interpret such behaviour as meaning 'let's find a solution'.[12] He is unable to stand back and listen and she experiences his behaviour as 'controlling'. Obviously, both men and women are caught up in these confusions and sometimes find each other's behaviour both confused and confusing.

'Distancer–pursuer' relationships

These gender differences may contribute to a pattern in relationships which has traditionally been labelled the 'distancer–pursuer' relationship. This is another type of 'misfit' relationship. This type of relationship is typically one in which the woman pursues for closeness and the man pursues for distance. Typically, the woman wants to talk about problems and feelings, and have physical closeness that does not always involve sex. The man may be more interested in doing things together and sexual closeness than talking about feelings and cuddling. Over time, the female partner tries harder to get what she wants and the male partner, feeling pressured, distances himself from her. A similar pattern may be set up where he pursues her harder for sex and she resists his pursuit. In one major study[13] this type of relationship was the most divorce prone and 80 per cent of the relationships in this category had the female as the pursuer and the man as the distancer, lending weight to the theory that gender differences may play some role.

Men often complain that they were quite unaware that their partner was unhappy in the relationship or marriage, much less contemplating separation. This has become more of an issue at separation, since more women have begun to initiate separation than men. The fact that some male partners feel that the decision to separate has been a unilateral decision on the part of their partners can contribute to a very conflictive divorce. Thinking about what has happened in a relationship in terms of intrinsic gender differences can help some men make sense of this situation. If women are more relationship-oriented and men more instrumental, this may well mean that there is more of a chance of them attributing different meanings to their marriage.

A man may consider that there are very few problems in the marriage or relationship, or if there are problems, he may consider that they do not justify such a drastic response as separation. His evaluation of the success of the marriage is likely to be on the basis of how well he is performing the traditional roles of providing, protecting and, if the couple have children, traditional fathering.

A woman's evaluation of marriage, on the other hand, is likely to be from a relationship viewpoint, with a negative assessment based on her partner's failure to communicate or show empathy. When she tries to talk with him about her concerns with the relationship and possibly her own dissatisfactions with her life, particularly if she is at home caring for children, she wants him to listen and to show understanding. He may take this as implied criticism that he is not 'pulling his weight' in helping her look after the children or he may suggest solutions and believe he has 'fixed the problem'. His partner might feel that her concerns have been dismissed. And so the cycle goes on. If she tries harder to make him understand, he may feel that she is pushing him and trying to control him. His response may be to withdraw still further by not listening or by staying away more. Alternatively, he may become angry and refuse to discuss the situation. This only makes her see his behaviour as domineering. If there is also a pattern where the male partner pursues her for sex, this may be further interpreted by her as pressure and control.

If and when they separate, she will feel that she has been telling her partner that there is something wrong for some time, while he genuinely will not have heard it in this way. Awareness and recognition of the misunderstandings that have occurred and of each partner's different understanding of what constitutes a good relationship can help to defuse this very natural tendency for both partners to blame the other and for the man, in particular, to feel that he has been unfairly treated over the separation. This feeling of unfairness comes from his experience of the separation as a unilateral decision on the part of his partner.

When men feel the separation has been unilateral

It is not unusual for men to feel that the separation has been unilateral and that their partner has not given the relationship 'a fair go'. This seems to be a common belief at separation in these types of 'misfit' relationships and one that the male partner needs to challenge. One of the tasks for these men is not to let feelings of anger and unfairness take over and form the basis of their response to their partner. This can involve them in fighting major battles for control of the children or alternatively withdrawing from the children's lives. Both strategies are motivated by a wish to punish the former partner, but both are likely to spell the end of fathering. This can easily happen unless he comes to an understanding of 'what went wrong' in his relationship. Being able to see that they both wanted different things from the relationship and that some of this is culturally driven can assist in arriving at such an understanding.

Dominant–submissive relationships

Traditionally, men have been socialised to be more dominant than women, to be more action-oriented and to see themselves as more rational and better at problem solving. For some men this leads to a belief that they should be in charge of their relationships. This contributes to a relationship pattern in which men assume a more dominant role and women a more submissive role. Some women may also subscribe to such beliefs, but with the radical changes to women's lives over the last two generations, women are less likely to accept such a relationship. Men who subscribe to this belief are frequently pursuing a first or second narrative type of relationship. Most women are not interested and are pursuing a more egalitarian relationship, one in which they are respected as an equal, no matter how they arrange their roles and responsibilities. Thus we have another 'misfit' relationship.

If this pattern has been established in a relationship, and if it is the female partner who ends the relationship, most men will interpret this as a challenge to their masculinity. On separation, their behaviour is often focused on demonstrating their continuing dominance over their partner. This makes it very difficult to form a parenting relationship because such relationships require the capacity to negotiate and this is virtually impossible if one partner is determined to assert their dominance, come what may.

A task for men in this position is to recognise that, while the relationship with their partner may have been one in which, for the most part, they were in charge, they are now moving into a situation of separation in which their partner rejects such a role definition as quite untenable. This means making a significant psychological shift almost overnight. While some men manage to accomplish this, others interpret their partner's action in terminating the relationship as a threat to their control and redouble their efforts to maintain the dominant position. Unfortunately, this effort may be channelled through the children and the man may pursue arrangements for the care of children that are based more on his own interests and on a desire to punish and control his former partner than on any wish to establish a viable parenting relationship. Les and Nancy illustrate this situation.

Les and Nancy had been married for eight years. Nancy has worked part-time since their daughter Sharon was born, despite being a highly qualified professional. She took a lower paying position in her profession to have more time to spend with her daughter. They also have a son, Liam, aged six. If she had not remained at home with her children, she would probably be in a similarly responsible and well-paid position as her husband, Les. Les became involved with another woman and Nancy decided to separate when Les would not terminate the relationship. The affair was longstanding and Nancy moved out of the house.

Les has a responsible professional position that involves him working late and being away frequently. He earns a very good salary. Les wants Sharon and Liam to live with him half-time, despite the fact that for a good part of the time they will be at his place, he will be away overnight or working late. His plan is to employ a housekeeper.

Nancy is extremely distressed by this and has pleaded with him to come to a more sensible arrangement in which she continues to care for the children after school and during the week. She thinks that Les should have the children when he is not working and she is willing to be flexible about this. She will also be more flexible if Les will change his working schedule, but Les sees no reason to do this. Their discussions usually end with Les haranguing Nancy, threatening not only to take Sharon and Liam away from her but also to make sure she gets none of the money from the sale of the house.

Because he has earned the most money, Les believes that he should get the major share of it.

The children are also becoming distressed. They have always been close to their mother. Their relationship with their father is more distant, mainly because he has been much less involved as a parent. He now prevents them from ringing their mother when they are with him and makes disparaging comments about Nancy in front of them. Nancy is afraid that Les will get the children for half the time. She feels intimidated by Les, but this is not a new feeling. Les was the one in charge of the marriage. Nancy has always felt one down. Les has been particularly disparaging about her work and she feels that he sees himself as superior to her both at home and at work. He demonstrates this by subtle put-downs about her work and her lack of ambition. Nancy is not afraid that Les will be physically violent to her but she does find it hard to stand up to him and have him take her views seriously. She is frightened that she will be disadvantaged legally because she cannot afford to employ a top solicitor. Les has already employed a top-flight solicitor whom he knows through his work.

Les continued to try to punish Nancy for her decision to move out and for her temerity in challenging his control of the relationship by pursuing a parenting arrangement with her that was clearly not in Sharon's best interests. He refused to go to counselling or mediation to try and resolve the situation through negotiation. Nancy clung to the belief that it could be sorted out through counselling or mediation, although this was highly unlikely given the power discrepancy. It was only when Nancy got herself a good solicitor, and Les learnt that if he went to court he was unlikely to succeed in his request that the situation was resolved. However, Les and Nancy were not able to evolve a cooperative parenting relationship. Nancy has tried to support Les's involvement as an active parent when he is available, but Les has taken a further promotion and now spends more than half his time in another city, where he is in a new relationship. His contact with Sharon is sporadic.

Violence and ideas of ownership

Sometimes, there are more dangerous ideas about gender operating both during the relationship and at separation. These ideas are not so much a product of confused and confusing messages about gender roles and gender differences as they are the result of an extreme male socialisation that can have a devastating effect on the lives of women and children. These ideas, such as ownership of women, women's inferiority and the right to use physical force and violence to get one's own way, are sometimes seen as a reversion to the assumptions of the first narrative that women are 'different and not equal'.

Extreme ideas about gender contribute to the formation of relationships in which men use power to control and dominate women, who conform through fear. There is good evidence to suggest that much of this behaviour is learnt through male role modelling and male socialisation in peer groups. There is also some evidence to suggest that men who use violence have experienced disruptions in their attachment relationships in childhood, leaving them anxious or fearful about relationships in general. This contributes to their controlling behaviour, since the more they control the situation the more they can avoid confronting what makes them anxious about the relationship. But, regardless of the origins of the dynamic, such relationships frequently present specific issues on separation that need very careful handling and professional intervention.

Of all the constraints operating at separation, the notion of ownership of one's partner is potentially the most destructive. We are not talking just about power struggles that can happen in every relationship from time to time. We are talking about relationships where one partner, usually the man, controls from such a position of power that his partner must remain in a position of subordination in which she is frightened to stand up for herself or her children. The man usually exercises control through intimidation and fear. Once a pattern of violence has been established, just the threat of more violence is often enough to get his partner to conform. If she does stand up for herself, she is likely to be physically abused.

Although the legal situation has changed dramatically over the past 150 years, beliefs that marriage, or for that matter cohabitation, somehow magically bestows the right to control one's partner are still pervasive. These beliefs are directly implicated in the use of violence in relationships and function to control the female partner and define the man in the superior position. At the extreme, these beliefs can lead to a man killing his partner (separation is the most dangerous time for spousal murder) and continuing harassment of the female partner long after the relationship is over. For the man himself, such beliefs make it well nigh impossible to build a new life after separation because he is unable to let go of what he sees as his property—the former partner or wife.

When ideas of ownership drive the male partner, it makes co-operative parenting after separation not only extremely difficult but also, in some circumstances, impossible and undesirable. Cooperative parenting cannot exist where there is violence or where there are major power and control issues. Ultimately, cooperation depends on developing a level of trust that is impossible to establish when fear is present. The safety of women and children must be put first. This may mean taking out a Domestic Violence Order and limiting contact with children to supervised arrangements until there is demonstrable change on the part of the father. But even supervised contact may not be appropriate if children are very fearful. In these situations, it is important to seek assistance to ensure that family members are safe and children assisted to deal with their fears and any anxieties resulting from their experiences.

In this chapter, we have looked at how ideas about gender influence men and women's relationships and decisions around parenting after separation. The key points are that changes in these ideas at an institutional and cultural level have not necessarily been followed by changes at the personal and behavioural level and that often demands for more egalitarianism in relationships are unsupported by necessary policy developments. As a result, men and women are confronted with many confusions and ambiguities. An understanding that all this confusion is not the result of personal inadequacy, but a product of rapid cultural and institutional change, which has left individuals running to catch up, can help parents to put aside their hurts and pain and concentrate on building a cooperative parenting relationship for the sake of their children.

6

Ideas about separation: Some common confusions

The legacy of various 'misfit' relationships is only one factor influencing how we organise our separation. Ideas about what should happen on separation also 'kick in' either at or before the actual separation. Here we discuss some of these ideas and locate them in the context of the three narratives. As we discuss these ideas, we see how they also interact with issues at separation that result from specific 'misfit' relationship patterns.

Conflict in beliefs over post-separation support for children

Until quite recently, the community was regarded as having an obligation to support women and children in the absence of a father. The establishment of the Child Support Agency marked a change in public attitudes and public policy. Partly, this was an outcome of a shift to neo-liberal views emphasising the responsibility of the individual, but it also fitted very well with the third narrative emphasis on parents' obligations to their children. The Child Support Agency was set up to enforce the financial obligations of parents,with this principle overriding all others, except in cases of violence and abuse. The duty to provide for children is enforced regardless of whether parents have contact with their children and whether or not one's former partner is in a new relationship in which the new partner also contributes to the family household. The clear intention is to enforce parental (mainly male) financial responsibilities to children. Most children are resident with their mothers and far more men than women pay child support.

While this principle of parental responsibility seems to have been accepted as an abstract principle (most people would agree that they should support their children), it is clear that some separating parents make exceptions according to their personal situation. Although one could analyse the issues and conflicts about child support on separation from a gender perspective, and although gender clearly plays some role, it is also the case that many of the issues and conflicts are the result of the structure of the situation. The fact that personal issues are being dealt with through bureaucratic channels can exacerbate the conflicts normally attendant on marital break-up. Part of the problem may be that decisions are imposed without reference to individual situations—a set formula is used with limited means of introducing flexibility, except by way of application to the Child Support Review Office for a review of the child support assessment. Administrative assessment and collection takes decisions out of the hands of individuals and may result in less ownership of the decision and a feeling of lack of control over the situation. If one or both parents are still very hostile towards each other, the timing of the child support request can get caught up in their battles and further exacerbate the troubles.

While some research has suggested that payment of child

support is more likely when fathers see their children,[1] other studies suggest that ability to pay is also an issue.[2] Currently, there is a significant debate in Australia about the links between child support and contact. While it seems to be the case that the two are linked, the connection is not straightforward. The links are mediated by factors such as 'the pre-separation relationship status of the parents, the quality of the relationship with the other parent, the age of the children, the physical distance of the non-resident parent from the children, the presence of a new partner, the presence of children from a new relationship, employment status, income and a sense of personal control'.[3]

We are going to concentrate on looking at just a few of the above factors, particularly those related to the quality of the relationship between the parents and a related sense of personal control. The argument is that if there is a positive relationship between parents and each feels as though they have a sense of control over their lives, then this optimises the chance of child support and contact working well.

One study found that non-payment of child support was linked in some fathers' minds to the following factors: whether or not they had on-going contact with their children; whether or not they believed the child support was being spent on their children and whether or not the resident parent had re-partnered and the new partner was contributing to the household.[4]

When payment of child support is linked in parents' minds to contact, it seems that it is often a basic criterion against which they assess the fairness or otherwise of their separation agreement. These parents (usually fathers) often see child support payments as leverage to maintain consistent contact. Alternatively they use their lack of contact to justify their non-payment. Some parents (usually mothers) see payment of child support as a basic criterion for allowing contact, and will withdraw contact if child support is not paid or is irregular.

For some separated fathers who feel on the edges of their children's lives, payment of child support becomes a channel through which they can assume some control. They may use it to feel more involved in parenting—to bargain for more contact, or to direct how it is spent. Some fathers believe that the mother is spending the child support on herself rather than the children. In this instance, fathers do not make the connection that the welfare of their children is intrinsically connected with the welfare of those most immediately concerned with looking after them. For many of these fathers their sense of control over their life has reduced dramatically since the separation. Often, they may believe that their former partner is responsible for this.

A mother will usually resist these attempts at control. She may believe the father no longer has a right to a say in these matters. It feels as though he is still trying to run her life just when she is trying to be more autonomous. Paradoxically, she too may feel as if she has little control over her own life. Some women may also believe that they are carrying the bulk of the child-rearing load and that this entitles them to a greater say in their children's lives.

Given that both parents feel a lack of control and given their different beliefs, she is likely to find his efforts to become more involved as intrusive. Feeling victimised, the father may attempt to withdraw child support and/or intensify his efforts to be recognised as a parent on his terms. And so the battle for control continues. And yet what both parents want is legitimate. Mothers who are the resident parent need regular child support while non-resident fathers want to be more involved in their children's lives. The problem seems to lie in misguided beliefs about how to achieve this that entrench battles for control and leave both parents feeling disempowered. In some instances, it is a replication of the battles they fought when they were together.

In the preceding situations, the parents involved are not able to separate their relationship with, and responsibilities to, their children from their hostile relationship with each other. Indeed, they are continuing the battle. This lies at the heart of parenting after separation—the ability to disentangle the relationship from parenting. This is often a challenge for men and women and the payment or non-payment of child support, or withholding contact, seems to provide a platform for continuing the fight.

When parents re-partner, the issue of equity between households can also become a cause for dispute. This can be the case even if there has been previously little dispute over these matters. This is because some parents believe that child support should be adjusted according to household income. They may also be faced with a situation in which they perceive their old family is better off than their new one. This may be particularly the case, if the father is the non-resident parent and has children by another relationship or is supporting children from his new partner's old relationship. However, child support policy in Australia assumes that both parents will honour their financial responsibilities to their children, regardless of their living arrangements. These types of situations can be very difficult. Indeed serial family situations pose the greatest challenge to child support reform development in Australia and elsewhere.

Finding a way through the conflict

Many of the problems and conflicts over child support are a result of conflicts about what people think are the right and proper ways to organise a separation and what public policy requires us to do. However, parents who want to parent cooperatively after separation, and who are caught up in some of these conflicts, often find it helpful to examine their motivations very carefully. Many of the exceptions to the overriding principle of parental responsibility that some parents use to excuse themselves from paying child support are concerned with their former partner's behaviour: she is refusing contact or making it difficult; she is spending the money on herself or she has enough money now that she has re-partnered. Behaviour of this kind may be real enough, but the real questions are how much does our own behaviour, our refusal to pay child support or denial of contact, reflect a desire to control our former partner and how much is it 'tit-for-tat' behaviour? In this situation, 'children become "pawns" in a power struggle between parents in which the pieces traded are contact and child support'.[5]

If parents are genuine in their desire to put their children's interests first, they will not respond to the other parent by making contact difficult or by withdrawing child support because, of course, that simply means it is the children who are harmed. This does not mean that the other parent's behaviour is justified, just that two wrongs don't make a right. In fact, many parents have found that one of the best ways of sorting out dilemmas concerning payment of child support and child contact is to break the link by deciding not to play the tit-for-tat game. They pay child support regardless of whether contact is difficult. They allow contact, regardless of whether they receive child support. Complaints about non-payment by the father or about the mother making contact difficult can then be dealt with as complaints in their own right. It becomes more difficult for the partner who is not allowing contact or not paying child support to maintain a righteous stance when the other partner is doing the right thing. When one parent refuses to play the game, the opportunity arises to shift the dynamics of the parent's relationship, allowing for the possibility of change and transformation into a new way of parenting.

Cameron and Denise illustrate this point (see box):

Cameron and Denise have been separated for three years. Denise has not worked since the children were born but she is retraining to return to nursing next year. They have two children—Justin, 6 and Gemma, 9. Cameron is supposed to have contact every second weekend and one evening a week. Changeover times are difficult. Denise and the children are sometimes not at home when he calls to pick them up. Other times, she says they are ill or it is someone's birthday. In fact, he probably sees the children about one in every three times it is his contact time. Cameron has tried to negotiate picking up the children from school but Denise, so far, has not agreed to this arrangement. Cameron is quite a few months behind in his child-support payments. He has been behind ever since they separated. Denise finds it hard to make ends meet and is very angry with Cameron over his non-payments. She feels that the Child Support Agency is not doing its job. Cameron is just as angry at his lack of contact and the continued hassles over child support. He had a period of unemployment recently and he thinks that the Child Support Agency has got his assessment wrong.

Cameron is very unhappy with life generally. He misses the children and he regrets the separation, but he knows there is nothing he can do about it now. Recently, he noticed that a group for men to discuss post-separation issues was being run in his area. He decided to attend, but told no one about it, because he felt slightly embarrassed at asking for assistance. He found the group incredibly helpful. He took note of some of the things that seemed to work for other men. He decided to try to sort things out with the Child Support Agency and made arrangements to catch up on his payments. He made arrangements to talk to Denise and let her know what he was doing. He apologised for making things difficult but he did not demand or ask that she make contact more regular. He saw her in a neutral place and only for a brief period of time to discuss the changes. When he did have the children he took good care of them. He stopped undermining Denise as a parent and, when it came to the children's birthdays, he rang Denise and asked if there was something they really needed. As there was not much money to go round, Denise found it very helpful that he was going to buy all the gear for Gemma to learn to swim for her birthday.

It took time for Denise to come round and Cameron found it difficult to sustain his supportive behaviour. It was hard to maintain such a positive stance with Denise, not knowing how she would respond. The group helped him in this respect, and he was able to contain his anger and urges to undermine Denise. Eventually, Cameron asked Denise if they could go to a family counsellor or child-focused mediation to sort out a better plan for the children. This coincided with a job offer for Denise. She was clear that returning to work would really ease the financial situation. However, she would be required to work most Friday nights. Cameron offered to have the children.

Cameron decided to take the risk and try to break the cyclical relationship with Denise. He decided he would pay child support regardless of whether Denise complied with the contact order. His behaviour helped to break the cycle and establish a new way of relating. He became open to thinking differently about his position and this gave him new solutions to consider.

What are the implications for cooperative parenting after separation? Cooperative parents wishing to arrive at a creative solution will usually be active in negotiating their own agreements. Cooperative routes, such as mediation or some combination of solicitors and alternative dispute resolution seem to work better for them, as a cooperative route allows them more influence and ownership over their parenting agreement. We discuss these more cooperative ways of reaching agreements in the next chapter. As we have seen, the quality of the parents' relationship is vital to making residence and contact work, and it certainly seems to play a role in how non-resident parents feel about paying child support. If both parents feel that they have been active in reaching agreement and they feel it is fair, that also assists both of them to feel that they have a sense of control over their lives—that neither one of them is pushing the other one around.

Notions of fault and blame

Our three stories of modern marriage have one thing in common: they all share the assumption that couples who conform to the standard expectations demanded by their particular narrative will be able to maintain a successful relationship, irrespective of the circumstances they confront. This means that it is almost impossible to avoid notions of fault and blame when relationships are less than successful or break down. Partly, this is a matter of attributing guilt for what has gone wrong in the relationship to the other party. The courts no longer support such attributions, but they remain central to many couples' public and private understandings of the situation in which they find themselves. Partly, it is a matter of feelings of responsibility on the part of one or both partners that they have contributed to the failure of their relationship and the repercussions for their children. When parties to a separation focus all their energy on blaming each other or themselves, it makes it extremely difficult for them to develop parenting strategies based on mutual cooperation in the interests of their children.

The attribution of guilt

'No-fault' divorce was introduced in Australia in 1975. It is now the basis for the dissolution of marriage in a large number of Western countries, taking the state out of the business of allocating fault and blame and assigning it to a neutral stance in relation to private matters in marriage. In Australia, divorce is based on one or both partners wanting to separate. There is only one ground for divorce and that is the irretrievable breakdown of the relationship. There is only one way of establishing that irretrievable breakdown has occurred and that is to prove that the partners have lived separately and apart for 12 months, interrupted by not more than one period (not exceeding three months) of getting back together. Previously, it had to be proved that one partner was at fault through such behaviour as adultery, cruelty or desertion. The introduction of the *Family Law Act* in 1975 signified a cultural shift towards the third narrative. However, cultural notions of blame and fault are so traditionally entrenched that they still persist in the personal behaviour of many separating couples.

Blaming our partner for the end of a relationship or marriage can be seen as almost a normal part of the emotional process of separation. In many instances, it is precisely because we assign fault and blame in our relationships that we end up separating. At separation, these ideas often come out into the open for the first time and the cycle of fault and blame may intensify. Part of coming to terms with separation involves not letting ideas of fault and blame take over and push us about. We allow these ideas to take over for a number of reasons. It is simpler to blame our partner than to look at what went wrong with the relationship as a whole, because it means that we don't have to examine our own role in the separation. Attributing fault and blame allows us to justify our behaviour in the eyes of the world, especially those of our family and friends.

When notions of fault and blame were given institutional support through fault-based divorce, they gained an external force that legitimised not only the normal tendency to assign blame as part of the private process of separation but also the public process. Fault and blame were assigned publicly and privately and the idea that there was someone to blame was reinforced through the interaction of public and private processes. We all knew that marriages broke up because one partner was cruel to the other, one partner deserted the other or one partner committed adultery. There was always an identifiable 'bad' partner.

This notion of assigning fault is still very ingrained, even though as a society we realised more than 25 years ago that assigning fault legally did little to assist positive separations. In fact, it did just the opposite. It kept couples locked together in misery and conflict and adversarial processes.

But, culturally, we still support the attribution of blame and fault by other means. When a famous couple separates, the media go into a frenzy about which one is to blame and which one has employed the best lawyer. There is endless speculation over who will get the house, the children and the most money. Separating couples still get caught up in publicly trying to justify their behaviour. Usually, this involves laying the blame on the other person.

Not only do separating couples wish to justify their behaviour publicly, but family and close friends frequently demand it of them. This demand for blame can be very distressing for children and may start a vicious cycle that cuts across the potential for co-operative parenting. It can keep people stuck in their relationship, unable to move on and negotiate new ways of working together to parent their children. Family and friends get more and more involved in assigning blame and positions become more and more publicly entrenched. Once positions have solidified, with family and friends enlisted as backers of the two protagonists, it is harder to pull back or back down. Anger and blame dominate the relationship, allowing little room for cooperation.

Accompanying notions of fault and blame are ideas of reparation: that somehow the partner who is identified as the one responsible for the 'breakdown' of the relationship must pay for their misdeeds and must balance the books for their failure to stick to the contract. This desire for reparation can be a public symbol of vindication of our role in the break-up or it can be a real desire to punish the other partner. Sometimes, where there is a desire for revenge or reparation, one partner will fight to exclude the former partner from the children's life.

Leaving aside violent relationships, the disintegration of a relationship is always a complex process with many contributing factors. There are competing explanations of what went wrong, some of which are more helpful than others. The issue here is whether looking at separation from a blame perspective is useful or helpful.

Apportioning blame needs to be clearly distinguished from accepting responsibility for our own actions in the relationship. The two notions differ: in the latter, we accept responsibility for our own behaviour; in the former, we assign responsibility to the other partner, usually without any reference to our own behaviour. In most relationships that are experiencing difficulties, part of the problem is the fact that one or both parties see the other partner's behaviour as the cause of the difficulties. But concentrating on our partner's deeds or misdeeds, and getting sidetracked by desires for revenge only prevents us from looking at our own role in the situation. That, in turn, prevents us from making decisions about how we should get on with our own life and makes it more likely that we will repeat the same mistakes in our next relationship.

When we blame others for our problems, things will only get better if the other person changes and that, of course, is extremely unlikely when separation has already occurred. The more likely response is that our former partner will become defensive and find reasons to return the blame and bitterness. Both partners are likely to construct competing stories and narratives about their marriage. These stories will fit within cultural narratives about marriage in general. This feeds into a repetitive pattern, where you can see people still trying to change their former partners behaviour years after the separation. The obvious questions to ask are these: If you were unsuccessful in changing your former partner's behaviour while you were still together, why on earth do you imagine that you will be more successful now that you have separated? Don't you think you might have missed the window of opportunity for working through this matter?

When we get caught up in a vicious cycle of blame and fault-finding at the time of separation and divorce, we are behaving in a manner dictated by the second narrative. If we take it further and demand reparation, we seriously jeopardise our chances of setting up a cooperative parenting relationship after separation. Cooperative parenting means putting the reasons for separation aside or, at the very least, not letting them overwhelm us to such a degree that we cannot negotiate a new type of relationship as parents.

Feeling guilty

It is not surprising that many parents feel guilt at the time of separation. As noted earlier, separation and divorce are credited with causing all sorts of social evils by conservative pressure groups and some researchers. For many separating and divorcing couples, the way in which the debate about divorce is conducted leaves one or both of them feeling selfish and inconsiderate of their children's needs. Both men and women can feel that they have failed in their responsibilities towards their children. Such feelings tie in with and are reinforced by a more general societal belief that men and women who separate have failed to match up to what is expected of them. As separation is already a very bruising experience in which people often have to cope with rejection by their former partner, this wider social condemnation can often add to their feelings of inadequacy. Inherent in all three narratives is the belief that if you conform to the standard expectations demanded by the narrative, you will have a successful relationship. The automatic response is to blame oneself for not having measured up, not to question whether the demands imposed by the narrative are reasonable or even possible.

Just as some feelings of blame towards a partner are normal on separation, so are feelings of personal guilt. Guilt is a normal part of the grieving process. It is when these feelings are prolonged or overwhelm us that they become a problem, for the person concerned, the children and the parenting relationship itself. Sometimes, feelings of guilt paralyse people and prevent them from getting on with their lives. Not infrequently, parents who become paralysed by guilt are very devoted to their children. Such parents find it difficult to come to terms with the fact that they can no longer parent in the way they believe is best for their children or provide what they see as a 'normal family environment'—almost invariably conceptualised as a nuclear family of mum, dad and children.

Parents who are troubled by guilt tend to be perfectionists who believe they should be fully in control of all aspects of their lives. However, no one is ever fully in control of their own life, perhaps least of all in the process of a separation, and every perceived failure contributes to a self-evaluation that is negative and overly critical. This can make such parents prone to depression. Where this occurs, they are likely to be even less available to their children, since withdrawal is a major feature of depression. Sadly, this further reinforces their negative perceptions of their success as parents and contributes to difficulties in parenting and problems for children. When parents are depressed, it is hard to maintain a good relationship with children and the parent/child relationship may deteriorate.

Another common problem that occurs when parents are overwhelmed by guilt is difficulty in setting limits and boundaries for children. They concentrate on 'what they have done to their children' and try to make it up to them by being permissive. They find it hard to deal with normal childhood protests over limits or to take a firm stance on issues when children insist to the contrary. Their guilt over the separation and their beliefs about its long-term impact on the child overwhelm them. This type of parental behaviour can produce confusion in children and reinforce feelings of insecurity. As we saw in Chapter 2, an authoritative style of parenting seems to be more protective of children during separation. We know that all children will test the limits so, unless limits are set, children will go on testing to find out how far they can go. When children's behaviour is difficult to handle, it makes cooperative parenting more fragile, as parents are prone to blame each other for their children's difficulties.

Challenging personal guilt and blame can be difficult. It is vital to distinguish between taking responsibility for our part in the relationship and being worn down by guilt that is out of proportion to the reality of the situation. Taking responsibility allows us to examine our own role in the separation, to assess how our partner has contributed to it and to learn from the experience. It also allows us to challenge socially constructed ideas about relationships and parenting and to examine whether we really want to allow these ideas to influence our behaviour in future relationships.

Overwhelming guilt, however, builds on itself and, with each re-examination of our role in the relationship and our current parenting deficiencies, we feel guiltier and guiltier. We feel more and more of a failure. We look more at how to handle guilt in Chapter 7.

Ideas about family

Inherent in all our narratives and stories are ideas about what constitutes a 'proper' family. In our first narrative of modern marriage, the family was defined very broadly to include extended family, while in our second narrative the notion is narrowed to include only the marital couple and children. On divorce, according to this narrative, the family was viewed as 'broken' and one parent was more or less excluded. In the third narrative, the concept of the family is beginning to broaden again. Relationships with other kin, such as grandparents, are being emphasised because of what they can offer children and because of their role in supporting parents in bringing up children. Ideas about what constitutes a family on divorce are also changing with both parents being urged to continue to play a role in their children's lives after separation.

However, although there is greater acceptance of both partners remaining involved with parenting, we are still ambivalent about whether these types of separation arrangements really qualify as a family. It is almost as though former partners who parent together are in no-man's land, neither fish nor fowl. Stepfamilies and single-parent families seem to suffer the same fate. These types of families are more accepted than they once were, but they do not quite seem to make the grade—they are somehow 'second-best' compared with intact families.

There are many instances of these cultural confusions about what constitutes a family. One couple in a cooperative parenting agreement after separation were given no option by their children's school but to have one of their addresses registered as the children's main address. School notices could not be sent to two houses. Many step-parents find that schoolteachers refer to them by their stepchild's surname. We have not quite developed structures and methods to deal with these intricacies. Nevertheless, how we construct our ideas of what makes a family and how other people and relevant institutions in society support these ideas impact enormously on how we organise separation and divorce and other future relationships. It is interesting to note that earlier societies with extended family structures managed to develop precise ways of delineating complex family relationships. Their ideas about family were grounded mainly in the first narrative, where stepfamilies were relatively common because of the early death of mothers in childbirth. We find it difficult to cope with anything more complex than the assumptions built around the nuclear family.

Nina's concept of the family caused problems when separation occurred (see box):

Nina came for counselling because she was having disagreements with her former husband, Neil. Her nine-year-old son, Paul, was being more disruptive than usual. Nina had an agreement with Neil in which she had major care of their two children, Sarah, 4 and Paul. Paul actually wanted to spend more time with his dad and had talked to Nina about this. Nina felt it would disrupt his routine too much. Neil paid child support and had contact every second weekend. He was always punctual, paid the child support on time and looked after the children well during his contact time.

Nina experienced Neil as intrusive, although when we looked into this she began to see that many of his questions were just routine inquiries about how the children were doing—such as how the sports day went or which tooth had fallen out recently. Nina had disagreed with Neil about Paul spending more time with him and the subject had not been discussed further.

Nina was very concerned for Paul's welfare and she did not see that spending more time with Neil would be of any benefit. After exploring a number of factors connected with difficulties on separation and finding that none of them seemed to be of much relevance, she finally began to examine her idea of what or who was included in her definition of a family. It emerged that she saw a family as a mother, father and children and, to some extent, grandparents. She saw herself as having made 'a mess of things', not only for herself but also for her children and her parents, because she had separated. She felt she would only be in a real family again if she remarried. On separation, she saw the family as being constituted by her parents, herself and her children. Neil was excluded, as were his parents. As we looked more closely, it became clear that she tolerated Neil's involvement, but only to a certain degree and only because she felt she had no choice.

Paul's idea of a family was quite different. He drew his picture of a family; it included his dad and his other grandparents. However, he did not draw it in a way that suggested his mum and dad should get back together again. He was clear that this would never happen. Nina realised that Paul's idea of a family and hers were different and this had quite an impact on her. She realised that the way she was acting was being driven by a view of a family in her head that might not be the best model for her situation and for Paul.

She decided to try to be more inclusive of Neil as a parent and renegotiated the contact arrangement with Paul. She also invited Neil's parents to Paul's tenth birthday party after much negotiation with Neil. Paul was pleased to have both sets of grandparents at his party. They found it strange initially and were unsure of how to react but, by the end of the party, both sets of grandparents were talking together and playing with Paul and both agreed that this was incredibly good for Paul.

Nina's ideas about family were firmly grounded in the second narrative. However, the needs of her child and her former partner would have been better served by a parenting arrangement that took note of ideas from the third narrative. Somehow, they were stuck between the two. When Nina realised the differences between her ideas and Paul's about family, she was able to make the adjustment and allow everyone in the family to make the transition into a new way of relating that, eventually, seemed to fit better for everyone. Nina was unusually successful in managing to be so inclusive of Neil's family. Not all separating couples want to do this or are emotionally able to, but many do find it possible to create a wider family context for their children.

Nina's and Neil's situation also illustrates the impact of separation on grandparents (see box):

Both sets of grandparents were upset when Nina and Neil separated. Neil's parents were particularly concerned by the thought of seeing less of their grandchildren. They contacted Nina after the separation, but they felt she was very distant. Since the separation, their relationship with their grandchildren had been only on weekends when Neil brought them over. They regretted the loss of their previous free and easy relationship with their grandchildren and the fact that the children no longer stayed with them. Neil's parents were in their mid-sixties and both had retired. They were concerned for Neil, who they felt was struggling to maintain his relationship with his children. They also felt he was paying too much child support, given that his contact with the children was minimal and he had so little say in their upbringing.

Nina's parents were concerned more about Nina than the children. They both worked but they felt they should be giving her more support. Although they had done some occasional babysitting, they had not taken on major responsibilities. They found they were spending more time at Nina's now. Nina's mother was taking time off work so that Nina could work when the children were ill and Nina's father had taken over many of the household repairs. They both felt rather tired and were thinking that one of them should take early retirement so they could support Nina more. They were angry with Neil and blamed him for the break-up but they were responsible about their anger and never talked to the grandchildren about their father. However, Paul asked them one day why they never saw his 'daddy'.

Both sets of grandparents were pleased but rather anxious about the changing situation. Nina's parents were worried about how they would react to Neil, and Neil's parents were anxious about Nina's reaction to them. They felt awkward meeting each other but they realised that, if this birthday party for Paul worked, it would be a great step forward. Although behaviour was stilted to begin with, with everyone anxious about saying the 'wrong thing', by the end of the party they knew they could manage it again. Although

Nina's parents were still angry with Neil over how they thought he had treated Nina, they witnessed his relationship with the children and this softened their anger. They were able to manage it and not let it interfere in the party. Nina was also reminded of her children's relationship with Neil's parents as she saw them relishing this time with their grandchildren. She began to think about letting them spend more time with them.

Although the notion of what constitutes a family in our society is becoming more elastic, as Nina's and Neil's story illustrates, certain ideas about family after separation appear to be deeply entrenched.

1. *Separation means the end of the family.* This seems to be a peculiarly adult notion, one that derives directly from the second narrative. From the point of view of children, all the people who were in their family before separation and divorce are still there. Separation may redefine how children relate to these people or how much they see them, but they are still important to them.
2. *Parents who cooperatively parent after separation are not a family.* Usually, other relevant people such as schoolteachers, doctors, other professionals and government agencies define one of the parents as the 'real parent' and the 'real family'. Other members of the family sometimes do this as well, particularly grandparents and uncles and aunts. Again, from the child's, and sometimes the parent's point of view, this is not the case. They may have rearranged the relationships in the family, with the parents no longer in an intimate relationship, but this does not mean they are no longer a family. Former partners who share parenting and financial responsibility for their children are challenging traditional views of families. Their children connect their households and they are connected by their responsibilities. Clearly, the parents have to negotiate new boundaries between the households and, in this sense, their

previous family has ended. But many parents today strive hard to preserve a sense of family for their children and see that they are connected through this web of relationships. One of the difficulties for this type of family arrangement is that we have no common name for it. Some researchers have named it the *bi-nuclear family*,[6] but until there is a more widely accepted name it will struggle to be recognised.

3. *Stepfamilies, also known as blended families or second families, are not real families.* This idea is based on the notion that family is defined through biological kinship. On first entering a stepfamily some children are very clear that their step-parents are not part of the family, because they include only biological relationships in their definition of a family. When couples separate, and one or the other repartners, it is vital that the notion of family expand to accept step-parents into this arrangement if parents want to continue to parent cooperatively. Interestingly, in our first narrative, all types of half- and step-relationships were seen as legitimate. The fact that we seem to have problems accepting stepfamilies as real families indicates that we still adhere to many second-narrative ideas about family, particularly the ideal of the nuclear family, despite knowing that this type of family now represents only a minority of all families.

Challenging ideas about what it means to be a family is particularly important when it comes to cooperative parenting after separation. We have seen that it is the quality of the relationships between children and parents and the parents themselves that is at the heart of cooperative parenting. Preserving relationships for children is fundamental to this way of parenting after separation. This is why the idea that 'the family is dead' when separation occurs is so toxic. It cuts right across any attempt to preserve those relationships.

Rethinking what it means to be a family is crucial. If parents can manage to think of themselves as a family, albeit a different one based on their parenting relationship, they are more likely to act in ways that protect this relationship than if they think of each other as someone who is no longer connected to them, an outsider. This sets a context, which is more likely to support a cooperative parenting arrangement.

Ideas about children

For the most part, we take our relationships with our children as fundamental givens. Most of us involved in bringing up children see the process as something entirely natural. We are not aware that much of what we believe about childhood and how we react to our children is socially defined. But, as we noted in Chapter 4, there have been massive changes in what it means to be a child over the last couple of centuries. How separating parents conceptualise what it means to be a child seems to play a central role in how they design post-separation arrangements for their children.

We no longer allow children to work (except in a minimal way) and we insist they attend school. These are two elements that define modern childhood that became routine features of children's lives only towards the end of the nineteenth century.[7] At about this time, governments in developed Western countries also began to protect children from maltreatment and abuse by people close to them. Over the course of the twentieth century, these protections were extended. More recently, notions of the 'child-centred family' and an increasing emphasis on the autonomy and personal integrity of the child have become more and more central to Western family law. The notion of the 'child-centred family' prioritises the interests of children above parents' rights and issues of fault in the breakdown of marriage. Children born outside marriage have also achieved equality with legitimate children in matters of inheritance and rights to parental support.

There is still wide variation among Western countries in the implementation of these recent rights. In Australia, we acknowledge children's rights to have a say in their own welfare and for parents to pay attention to their wishes on separation, as well as to have a continuing relationship with both parents. Some states acknowledge a child's right to divorce their parents in certain circumstances, and most states recognise children's rights to have control over their bodies under certain circumstances without their parents' knowledge or consent—for instance, the right to seek an abortion or to use contraception. In Australia, however, we have not yet gone as far as the Scandinavian countries, where it is illegal for schools to use any form of physical punishment and where parents are not allowed to smack their children at any age.

For many parents, these more recent changes, particularly those dealing with the child's rights to personal autonomy and integrity, are a major departure from how they themselves were brought up and how they personally view their relationships with their children and their responsibilities towards them. There is a sense in which the words 'children's rights' frightens parents because they feel that this means that the children will 'take over'. They will lose their authority as parents. But one study found that what children want when it comes to separation is not so much rights but a voice.[8] This means being listened to, respected and given information. They don't want to make the big decisions, but they do want to participate.

As noted in Chapter 4, some parents see these changes as challenging their traditional authority over their children. They see themselves as owning their children and having an inherent right to tell them what to do.[9] For these parents children are not autonomous beings in their own right. Other parents see the implementation of these rights as asking too much of children, expecting them to take on adult responsibilities way before it is appropriate. They feel that adults have a duty to protect children from the realities of life. Childhood should be a happy and carefree time. Letting children have a voice at separation threatens this concept of childhood. They believe it increases children's vulnerability and their sense of anxiety about the world.

But underlying these beliefs about the traditional authority of parents over children and about protecting vulnerable children from the adult world are other more fundamental notions. These notions—that adults know what is best for children and that parents, always act in their children's best interests—have a strong potential to conflict with and undermine children's rights and concerns, particularly on separation. We have two value systems operating at the same time. We have acknowledged that children have rights, but children are also seen as minors. Adults are assumed to be able to judge what is in a child's best interests better than the child itself.[10]

Challenging beliefs about protection

When parents give children only minimal information about the separation and little or no voice in the decision making about arrangements they are frequently acting from the belief that they are shielding their children from the pain of the separation. These parents may be very worried about their children and the impact of the separation on them. They believe and hope that that they are keeping their children safe by shielding them from the traumas and they may believe that this will protect the quality of their relationship with their children in the long term. But we know that children do notice what is happening in their families and they often feel very frightened and alone. The intended protection often results in more distress and parents and children's relationships can become problematic.

It seems that for parents to protect the quality of their relationships with their children during the upheaval of separation, they need to communicate more, not less. This communication is actually protective of children, because then they know what is happening in their lives and they have the opportunity to make sense of it.

Parents who want to parent cooperatively at separation think about their ideas about protecting children and what this means. Because 'protection' so often equates with this idea of 'shielding' and this means communicating less (if we don't tell children things it won't affect them), many parents are at a loss as to how to talk with their children about separation and how to give them a voice. This is new to them. They would automatically do the opposite and they may feel 'they are not up to the task'.

The situation may be further complicated if they are intensely concerned about the impact of the separation on their children. Feelings of concern interact with feelings of inadequacy. They may not know what to do and they may fear that they will make things worse for the children. They may think it is better to say nothing. In these situations, parents might like to consider enlisting help. There are many excellent child-focused counselling and mediation services, with professionals trained to talk with children and build up a picture of the child's world. They can then feed this information back to the parents. The children might also benefit from attending a children's program where they can talk about their concerns and learn strategies to help them deal with the separation. Just the simple act of going to one of these programs often transforms communication between parents and children. Children feel that participation in the program gives them permission to talk with their parents as their parents have encouraged them to attend the program and they learn through the program how to 'name' some of what is happening to them.

Challenging beliefs about parental authority

Giving children a voice at separation can seriously challenge some parents' beliefs about both their parental authority and the place of children in the family. This is such a fundamental belief for many parents that it is very difficult for them to even consider that it might not be helpful in the situation of separation. It is a radical departure from how they were bought up and they fear the consequences of parenting differently. A belief in giving children a voice (or their right to have a say in decision making) and a belief in the absolute right of parents to have authority over their children are in many ways in opposition to each other. The first requires that we take children's views and concerns seriously and be prepared to moderate what we think is best for them, while the second privileges adults' views and devalues negotiation. This is a good example of the radically different ways of thinking about children built into our different narratives.

If we are going to give children a meaningful voice at separation, this requires that we really listen to our children. Being able to really listen means being able to empathise, to relate to what is happening for the other person. When this happens, the other person feels understood. This reinforces our trust in the relationship. It is often very hard for parents to fully appreciate what is happening for their child at separation for a number of reasons. In Chapter 2, we discussed how children and parents are frequently in a different place at separation. Some parents are preoccupied with their own distress; some are captured by new relationships, while others are so preoccupied by guilt that they have to protect themselves from their children's pain. Some parents have to challenge their own beliefs about protection. All of these factors can mitigate against us listening to children. We are in such different places that we cannot put out ourselves in their place.

In addition, children's understandings of separation and divorce are often poles apart from their parents'.[11] This difference in family members' stories also forms a barrier to listening because each parent may believe that their story or account is the one 'true' story. This is a normal part of what happens at separation. Each parent and each child has their own understanding of why the relationship fell apart and how they and other family members experience it. We discuss this discrepancy between family members' understanding of why the separation occured in the next chapter. However, it is often hard to appreciate that children's understandings, while being different from ours, do not invalidate them. They are just different. Truth is not the issue. It is very hard to hear a different version of the same event if we believe that our version is the real 'truth'.

Yet despite many of the above barriers to really listening, many parents do manage to hear their children's stories and take their concerns and views into account. However, it is almost impossible for parents who believe that their authority is being challenged to even make space to give their children a voice. They believe they already know what the separation feels like for their children and they know what is the best solution to help children move to a new, better place. They see themselves as the expert on their children, not children as the experts on themselves.

We talk more about how to listen to children in the next chapter but it is fundamental to good listening, that we examine our own beliefs. When we are able to listen to children, it brings home to us that there are more then two players in a separation. This in turn makes it very difficult to persist with solutions that do not take their concerns into account.

In these last two chapters we have examined the role that different narratives or stories about marriage and separation play in how we organise parenting after separation. In Chapter 5 we looked at misfit relationships and some of the potential consequences for cooperative parenting after separation. We saw that there were many different and competing stories about what is best for children on separation when viewed through the lens of gender. In this chapter we looked at how fault and blame on separation are built into the expectations of family and friends about divorce, even though these notions no longer play any part in divorce proceedings. We have also charted the impact of our beliefs about family relationships. Contrasting these stories of modern marriage, we see that ideas about family and childhood are socially defined. Some of these ideas allow us more room to manoeuvre than others when it comes to cooperative parenting.

In the final two chapters we look in more detail at strategies for cooperating after separation and at techniques we can try when parenting together does not seem to be going according to plan.

7

Building a creative parenting relationship

Building a cooperative parenting relationship after separation is like building a house. There are many ways of building it and a variety of innovative designs that can be chosen. It is even possible to 'mix and match' and create our own design. We may have enough money and time in the beginning to build a large, solid house or we may have only enough resources to build a prefabricated cottage. The house may be constructed with a view to making additions later on, or it may be designed to meet most of the owner's foreseeable needs now, but with enough versatility to make internal changes down the track.

The building process may go reasonably smoothly with little runover in cost and time or it may encounter all sorts of obstacles and frustrations along the way, with some of the workers going on strike, building materials costing more than was budgeted for, the finished product not quite as initially advertised and completion much delayed. But whatever type of house is built, it must conform to a minimum standard. Otherwise, it is unlikely to remain standing and those occupying it are in danger of being hurt.

This metaphor resonates for many parents trying to build a cooperative relationship after separation. Sometimes there are enough personal resources for the parents to build a fairly solid agreement from the beginning with a minimum of disruption. These tend to be the couples who have already cleared away the debris of their earlier marital relationship. The resources they possess include a reasonable level of trust and confidence in each other as parents, a capacity to communicate and to focus on the needs of their children, and a degree of concern for each other's well-being, even though they are no longer partners. They realise that their children's well-being depends to a large extent on the well-being of both parents.

Other parents have more of a struggle to build a cooperative relationship that works reasonably well for everyone in the family. The collapse of the relationship may have affected their trust and confidence in each other as parents, or there may always have been deficiencies in this aspect of their parenting. Varying levels of conflict and anger may cut across their capacity to communicate and focus on their children's needs.

Often, so little goodwill is left towards each other that there is a scarcity of resources from which to fashion a cooperative parenting relationship. Under these circumstances, the first task is to find sufficient resources from which to construct a basic agreement (a prefab, kit house or studio flat), which may be embellished later when they have accumulated more resources. They first have to clear away enough of the debris of their previous relationship to allow space to construct this agreement. The more debris they clear away, the more scope there will be to build further on the agreement. Alternatively, they might never wish to extend the arrangement, because they find that the present structure works perfectly adequately.

With parents who have to generate resources and sort through enough wreckage to allow construction work to begin, the building process may take some time and their ideas about what to build may change in the process. The kind of resources they have to generate include reduced levels of conflict, increased confidence and trust between them, more positive communication that allows for a minimal working cooperative relationship, and the ability to handle their emotions. For some people—depending on the amount of debris left from the relationship—finding these resources may require assistance with coming to terms with the end of the relationship (in terms of our metaphor this can be likened to building advice).

Whatever type of relationship is created by the parents—a maximum or minimum cooperative relationship, or something in between—building codes are available to help build firm foundations for the relationship. Later on in the construction process, parents may again encounter critical decision points and resolving these will either strengthen or destabilise the foundations. So it is crucial to build firm foundations with a real potential for standing firm against earth tremors further down the track.

The meaning of creative cooperative parenting

In Chapter 3 we identified five essential building blocks for creative parenting.

1. An understanding that our relationship with our former partner is a crucial aspect of the relationship with our children.
2. A focus on the well-being of children.
3. Setting up workable contact and residence arrangements.
4. The ability to set aside anger and bitterness and not allow these emotions to drive our behaviour.

5. Taking one thing at a time.

Components 1 and 4 highlight the central dilemma that must be resolved to achieve cooperation. This dilemma is straightforward—former partners need to learn to tolerate negative feelings towards each other, while at the same time acknowledging the other's positive virtues as a parent.[1] Resolving this dilemma is fundamental to clearing away the debris of the marital relationship and requires separating the roles of partner and parent. This is difficult to achieve in our culture, where the two roles are closely entwined. Most counsellors and researchers working in this area agree that this is a fundamental dilemma which has to be resolved if parents are going to work together cooperatively to bring up their children.[2,3] In Chapter 2, we discussed establishing a business type relationship between separating parents. This type of relationship has clear boundaries and clear goals and for its success usually relies on both parents being able to put aside their former intimate relationship.

Separating these roles is even more difficult because former partners have to cope with two opposing demands on the relationship. The first demand is to increase personal distance and reduce interaction with each other after their earlier intimate relationship, while the second is to work together to protect the cooperative elements from that relationship that still exist, or to build cooperation where it has not existed before. The second demand depends to some extent on building effective communication, based on trust and some degree of mutual tolerance. These are key elements of relationship building. While communication may be limited in the early stages of separation, it must, nevertheless, be effective. The two processes make contradictory demands of us—to dismantle a relationship and to build it at the same time.

To cope with these different demands means that parties to a cooperative relationship must be able to tolerate uncertainty. That is because, although the ultimate goal is to do the best by the children, it is not clear at the beginning what that best might look like or what it might take to achieve it. We need to bring a degree of flexibility and inventiveness to solving the dilemmas of separation. Parents cannot handle uncertainty if they have only one way of thinking about problems and always reach the same conclusions. A strategy recommended by many professionals is to think about the relationship with the other parent as though it were a business arrangement. In most business relationships, the focus is on the present and the future and the parties are pragmatic in their approach to each other. There is clarity about what is to be achieved and a willingness to negotiate and compromise to achieve it. The possibility of developing a business-like relationship when parenting after separation arises when parents share the aim of doing what is best for their children and are willing to put their emotions to one side to bring it about.

The big problem for most couples, at least in the initial stages of separation, is that there are two tasks involved in establishing a cooperative parenting relationship and these tasks are potentially conflicting. One is fostering a pragmatic approach to parenting issues. The other is dismantling the pre-existing relationship of intimacy between the partners, if this has not already been done. The more conflict and distress involved in the separation, the greater the need to devote attention to this second task. If a building site is littered with debris, the construction firm has to clear some of the wreckage before it can begin the task of building anew. The more debris it clears, the more space it has to begin work, although it is not always necessary for all the rubble to be cleared before beginning to lay the foundations.

Dismantling an intimate relationship usually involves dealing with the immediate crisis (if there is one), learning to manage our emotions, taking time to mourn the end of the relationship, and coming to some understanding of how the relationship came to unravel. One of the gains in attending to the whole of the cooperative parenting equation (dismantling the old as well as constructing the new), rather than just one aspect of it, is that success in one area seems to reinforce success in the other. If we can organise one meeting in which we are able to maintain a business-like stance, no matter how cooperative or uncooperative our former partner is, it helps in coming to terms with the separation. And the more we are able to do to end the former relationship, the more we are able to be business-like with our former partner.

The decision to separate

As we have noted in Chapter 3, separations can be both highly organised and structured or they can be quite chaotic. Some couples take a long time to reach the decision, negotiating and planning over a long period of time. These parents, for whom the decision is more or less mutual, have a head start when it comes to extricating their couple and parenting relationship. They have already cleared away much of the debris of their past together. Some parents are just beginning to clear away the debris at the time of separation, while others continue to heap more and more debris on their relationship. For these parents, cooperative parenting is much more of a challenge. It is more usually the case that one partner initiates the separation and that this partner is more equipped to deal with it.[4] The less prepared partner may be thrown into chaos, although even the partner who initiates the separation may be surprised by the intensity of their emotional reactions. They especially may be confused at the amount of guilt they feel. This guilt can sometimes cause them to send conflicting signals to their former partner. It drives them to try and help their partner deal with the separation but the former partner interprets this to mean that they still care and may still want the relationship.

Chaotic separations are common. Separating couples are frequently overwhelmed by emotions and find it very hard to think and plan rationally. One of the partners may move out as the result of an angry episode, or discover that the other is having an affair. Sometimes the decision is reached after a long period of emotional ambivalence on the part of one partner. This emotional ambivalence may not be resolved with the separation. Some couples reunite and separate many times.

Ideally, the process of cooperative parenting begins at or before the separation but this depends on there being a good amount of order in the separation. The reality, however, is often very different. At separation, parents often are functioning automatically in an attempt to survive on a day-to-day basis, and parenting competence is diminished. It is only on reflection, when things have settled down somewhat, that they realise some decisions may need to be reconsidered.

It is worth remembering that only so much of the separation process is within one person's control. Separating partners are frequently in radically different places with regard to both the acceptance of the separation and understandings about why it has occurred. Therefore while one partner may want to adopt a more cooperative stance, the other partner may take time to reach a similar position. All we can do, if our partner is less inclined to be cooperative, is to help the children understand that the other parent is having a difficult time and maintain our own cooperative stance. It is always helpful to operate on the principle that two heads are better than one, but one is definitely better than none. One up is better than two down!

The ability to parent cooperatively takes time and needs room to grow. So it is important to be flexible and not to close off options prematurely by allowing problematic decisions to become binding. No matter how uncooperative a separation has been so far, it is always worth trying to turn it around.

Telling the children

Irrespective of the reasons leading up to the decision to separate, it is helpful if children are told about the separation in a way that helps them start to come to terms with it. The 'ideal' circumstances seem to be where the separation has been negotiated between the parents and they can sit down and tell the children together. This doesn't mean that the separation is necessarily a mutual decision—just that the partner who is more attached to the relationship acknowledges that if their partner sincerely wants to leave the marriage, there is no point in trying to force them to stay or to punish them for their decision.

We know from research on separation outcomes for children and from what children tell us of their experience of separation (see Chapter 2) that children:

- benefit from an age-appropriate explanation of why the separation is happening;
- want to know in simple terms what is going to happen to them initially;
- want to be reassured that both parents still love and care about them and that both will remain involved as parents;
- want the opportunity to ask questions of their parents and have some voice in the future arrangements of the family—but they don't want to be forced to do this;
- find other people, such as grandparents, helpful as supports during this time;
- find it easier to deal with the situation if parents start to normalise the situation by suggesting that it is one that many children face—lots of parents don't live together and lots of children have two homes;
- need time to adjust, just like adults.

We know that children find it difficult when:

- parents don't explain about the separation because they believe it is self-evident;
- parents explain about the separation, but do so in a way that blames the other parent, or give reasons that don't seem to fit with the child's experience of the parents' relationship;

- they are confused for a long period about what is going to happen to them;
- they only find out about the separation when they discover a parent has left the home and are unsure what will happen to their relationship with that parent;
- they have to witness and deal with their parents' conflicts at this time;
- they feel they have to take sides and are not disabused of this fact by both parents;
- they feel they have no control over what is happening;
- they are not able to ask questions of their parents;
- they feel they have to reverse roles and look after their parents.

We also know that children will be:

- *distressed and upset* by the fact of their parents' separation and that this may prevent some parents from giving them full information, because the parents find this distress hard to witness and deal with. However, children's distress is normal and healthy;
- *able to cope with their parent's distress*, despite parents being concerned about this. They realise that being sad is an appropriate response. However, parents being out of control and relying on children to help them deal with their emotions for any length of time is a difficult situation for a child.

If parents can manage to tell their children together, it sends the children a positive message about the separation—they are going to try to cooperate over this matter. It is a clear signal that the parents are still in control and are taking steps towards building a positive parenting relationship. If parents can't manage to tell the children together, it helps if they try to tell the children the same thing. It is not possible for many parents to tell their children together for all sorts of reasons. If this is the case, and parents focus on what the children need when they tell them separately, it will still be a helpful experience for the children.

Dealing with a painful situation

Parents often get distressed when they think they have mishandled a situation. However, measuring our actions against ideal standards can be a mistake if it disempowers us and increases our sense of failure. As we have seen, the area of separation and divorce is beset with confusions and conflicts over cultural expectations, personal behaviour, legal norms and public policies, stemming from contradictions between our three narratives. The fact that some parents take an adversarial approach (i.e. they fight about everything) from the moment of the decision to separate can easily be understood as a product of these confusions and conflicts. Other parents simply don't know how to talk to their children about what is going on and may be overwhelmed by their own pain.

Sometimes, the conflict involved in decision making at separation is so intense that one parent leaves to avoid making the situation worse. Sometimes, one parent is left to pick up the pieces. The other parent is not open to ideas about how to separate differently. Sometimes, people say things they later regret. This is the reality of separation for many people and parents need to go easy on themselves.

With the passing of time and the cooling of emotions, some parents regret the way in which the initial separation happened. They want to know what they can do now to ease the situation for the children and help them come to terms with the separation. When even only one parent feels like this, there is much that can be done to promote children's resilience. The first step that many parents take is to talk to their children about their regret at how the separation was handled. If one parent left in haste without telling the children, or one or both parents tried to enlist children to their side or were overly negative about the other parent, then parents can explain in simple terms how they were confused and not coping very well at the time. Some parents then find it useful to give the children an explanation of the separation and reassure them of their love. Some reassurance that they are going to try to do things differently also seems to help. Children are very forgiving of their parents and respond positively when their parents talk to them in this way.

Letting family and friends know

Once the decision to separate has been made, couples face the reality of telling family and friends. Many people in counselling talk about how difficult it is to tell other people and how much they wanted their family and, in particular, their parents to understand and be supportive. They felt it was a difficult enough decision to make without having to cope with disapproval from people close to them, on whom they could usually rely for support. Sometimes, family and friends know there are major problems, but some couples keep their difficulties to themselves or minimise them in public. Thus, the separation comes as a surprise to significant others. Sometimes, family and friends have already been enlisted in the couple's conflict and have formed alignments with one or other of the partners.

The decision to 'go public' marks a critical turning point for the couple.[5] As long as the decision remains private it seems less real, and there is always the possibility that one or other of the partners will change their mind. Once it is public, there is less chance of this occurring. How relatives and friends respond can also have an impact on the couple's chance of building a cooperative relationship. Only too often what they say exacerbates the situation, reinforcing animosities that are close to the surface at separation time. This creates more debris that needs clearing away before a cooperative parenting arrangement can be made. Friends and family who are genuinely concerned about parents and children at the time of separation need to be careful not to make the situation worse.

The circumstances surrounding the decision to separate have

an impact on how friends and family respond. If the separation is impulsive, or one partner leaves to live with another person, these actions are more likely to invoke censure than a separation that has been negotiated between the partners, in which it is clear the couple are trying to do the best for the children. However, as we have seen, extended family and close friendships are very important to children at separation. Close contact with family and other significant adults can help children cope much better with the separation by providing support and a place to talk, as well as a safe haven for children when parents are overwhelmed by their own emotions and find it hard to cope.

However, a number of situations can arise that interfere with this important supportive role. If grandparents and other family members such as uncles and aunts, as well as significant friends, become too critical of one of the parents, the positive impact that their care and support for the children can offer may be diminished. It will quickly become clear to children if family and friends take sides, creating further dilemmas for the children. These dilemmas are about conflict of loyalty. If grandparents or other relatives take sides, it is more than likely that one of the parents is also trying to enlist their children's loyalty. Instead of the children having an escape from this pressure, they are confronted with a double dose of loyalty strain.

A second problem may surface when grandparents, usually from the best of motives, become too involved with their separated adult child and grandchildren. A delicate balance is needed here. Extended family, particularly grandparents, can offer much needed and valued support, allowing the parent to regroup and establish the new family situation. But grandparents can also take on a renewed parenting role with their adult child, which gets in the way of that parent establishing a new family in its own right. This may not be much of a problem, unless it interferes with the parent's capacity to take responsibility and negotiate a positive separation. Sometimes, when grandparents become overinvolved, they encourage their adult child's negativity towards the other parent and support the exclusion of him or her from an ongoing parenting role. More frequently, they take over the role of the absent parent, leaving him or her increasingly marginalised.

A further problem can arise when grandparents are not supportive of the cooperative parenting arrangement itself. It is easy to understand how their negativity may arise. Grandparents are another generation removed and it is more than likely that their views on divorce and separation and care of children will be grounded in the second narrative we looked at. Their expectation may be that it is best for the children to live only with one parent and they may expect former partners to behave in a bitter fashion towards each other. They may believe that children will not be able to cope with the disruption of shared parenting.

Parents may not be able to convince grandparents of the benefit of cooperative parenting, but they can ask them to suspend judgment until they see how it works and they can insist that grandparents do not undermine arrangements concerning the children.

Finally, the nightmare of every grandparent and involved uncle and aunt is that they will be excluded from their grandchild's or niece's or nephew's life. In this case, the separation becomes a rejection of the family of the former partner. Unless the children spend a considerable amount of time with each parent, with that parent supporting them in continuing family relationships, children may lose significant relationships, as do grandparents and other family members.

So, when it comes to making the separation public, many couples have found how important it is to avoid enlisting significant others to their side, tempting though it might be. This can be achieved by being proactive and making it clear to family and friends that, despite being hurt and upset, they do not want to:

- fight over the children;
- expose the children to negative comments about the other parent;
- deprive the children of any significant relationships.

Grandparents and other significant people can help children to cope with separation by:

- containing any negative feelings they may have about the other parent and avoiding taking sides;
- helping their adult children to avoid taking adversarial positions by bringing discussions back to the needs of the children;
- being available to support the parent in a positive manner that does not involve taking over their life;
- providing support and a place for children to 'escape' from some of the home tensions, especially if parents are finding it difficult to manage their emotions;
- supporting decisions by the separating parents to parent cooperatively and reinforcing to the children that this situation happens to many children, thereby helping to normalise it for them.

When grandparents and other family and friends behave in these ways, they help to build a positive coalition that will support the cooperative parenting relationship. The more isolated the separating pair are from family and social support, or the more hostile this support is to their arrangements, the more difficult it is to establish a cooperative parenting relationship. For many grandparents and other relatives, it is a challenge to think flexibly and creatively about separation because thinking in these ways departs from many of their beliefs about how separation should be handled. However, many grandparents rise to the challenge and find they can make an important contribution to their grandchildren's welfare.

Clearing away the debris

When parents find it hard to act in ways that help to build a cooperative parenting relationship, they are often frustrated by the fact that they know what they want to do but are unable to put it into practice. Others are overwhelmed by sadness or rage and cannot see a way through. Such parents often find it useful, if they are already involved in either formal or informal negotiations, to slow down the pace of negotiations so they can take time to deal with emotional issues. By doing so, they reduce the risk of getting stuck with unwise decisions, or adding to the debris surrounding their former relationship by engaging in escalating negative interactions with their former partner. It is not unusual for problems between former partners to get worse for some time after the separation, possibly as a result of trying to come to terms with the end of the relationship. This is not the time to negotiate binding agreements.

Parents may also find themselves struggling with depression, grief or overwhelming anger. They feel it is as much as they can do to focus on the present, let alone making plans for the future. They may feel guilty about their children and be paralysed by feelings of responsibility. When parents feel like this, probably the most sensible step they can take to protect their children is to delay building an agreement and stay with temporary arrangements. Once they feel more emotionally in charge, they can return to or start the negotiation process.

If we look more closely at the central dilemma of cooperative parenting after separation—that is, learning to tolerate negative feelings towards our former partner at the same time as acknowledging their positive virtues as a parent—many parents initially feel overhelmed by the task. They take it to mean they must stop feeling negative about their former partner in order to be able to feel positive about them as a parent. This is a normal reaction and demonstrates how easily we are drawn into 'either/or' thinking as opposed to what is sometimes described as 'both/and' thinking. In our culture, we mainly see things as right or wrong, black or white—that is, we think in terms of polar opposites. From such a perspective, it is natural that anger and blame become a largely negative appraisal of the former partner's conduct. The logical consequence of this is to reject him or her completely. If they have been a 'bad' partner, they cannot be a 'good' parent. This exempts us from blame.

A more creative way of looking at what needs to happen is to take a 'both/and' perspective. In this view, it is perfectly possible for the former partner to be both a 'terrible' partner and a good parent. When we are not under stress, we find it relatively easy to tolerate ambiguity and to see and accept both the strengths and weaknesses in others and ourselves. We realise that people are complex and we relate to others as such. We find it easier to tolerate differences and to see the issues as differences between us. But, under stress, we tend to revert to a childish world peopled by goodies and baddies with no shades of grey—we cannot tolerate the complexity of trying both to love/admire and hate/despise the same person. Our natural response to this conflict is to try to eliminate it by shutting the other person out of our life: 'If only he were dead, or I did not have to see him, or I did not have to talk to him.'

It is very important for parents to make this distinction between their former partner's virtues as a parent and their problems as a partner. It is a natural stage of separation to feel hurt, upset and angry. For a while these feelings make the separation tolerable. The key is to learn to manage these feelings so that they do not interfere with building a cooperative relationship. Until feelings are at a manageable level, the couple will not have space to build the resources necessary to negotiate about parenting arrangements.

One way of managing these feelings is to minimise interaction with one another and make sure that any contact for the sake of the children is conducted according to formal rules. The more parents continue to interact in a negative fashion, the more debris they will heap on the pile and the longer it will take to clear it away.

Another way is for each individual to look at how they are managing their own feelings and to determine where they are in the grieving process. In Chapters 5 and 6 we discussed how the attribution of guilt, blame and fault can play a prominent role in keeping us connected in unhelpful ways to our former partner. Our perspective here is rather different. In this chapter we focus on developing strategies to handle these feelings in order to minimise their impact on cooperative parenting.

A grieving process

We can liken the process of disentangling an intimate relationship to grieving, something akin to the emotional transition that occurs when we mourn the death of a loved one.[6] For most people, there seem to be predictable stages which they go through before they can fully accept the reality of a separation. However, the timing and intensity of these stages vary. There are real similarities with the mourning process, but real differences too. Death is final and the partner can't be brought back, whereas separation involves one or both partners voluntarily choosing to leave, and there is always the fantasy of reconciliation. For some parents, separation also gives the prospect of a new beginning. As well as loss there is also hope.

The grieving process is almost never an easy one and parents can get stuck at many stages, particularly denial and anger.

Denial

Denial is likely to be a particular problem for the person who has been left. They may find it hard to believe that the relationship is really over and spend much of their time living in hope that their partner will return. Some denial is normal but it can be paralysing if it takes over and keeps us living in hope, despite all evidence to the contrary. It can prevent us from confronting the issue of why the relationship ended, from mourning it appropriately and from taking the necessary steps to lay it to rest. It may also keep those who have left a relationship more involved than they wish to be, since those who leave often feel guilty and sometimes try to ease the pain of their former partner. This sends all the wrong signals and tends to reignite hope.

When a parent responds to separation with denial it can interfere with cooperative parenting after separation. We know that children often fantasise about their parents getting back together again and that they need their parents to disabuse them of this if they are eventually to accept the separation. If one parent is bound up in the same fantasy as the children, this may reinforce the children's fantasies.

A parent in denial will frequently resist making formal arrangements for the children or finalising the legal aspects of the separation. In effect, life is put on hold for everyone concerned. Parents who cannot accept that the relationship is over are unable to move on and build a life in which they take responsibility for themselves. Sometimes, they come to rely heavily on their children for emotional support. This can overburden children who are, implicitly or explicitly, made to feel responsible for their parent's well-being.

Parents trapped in the denial process for any length of time may need to seek professional help or join a support group to help them move on. A problem, of course, is acknowledging what is happening. Parents often move from denial into depression and withdrawal, and it is only then that they realise something is really wrong. They become more withdrawn because it is impossible to get on with life. Some people recognise their reluctance to move on and they may also recognise the fear connected with it. Seeking professional support can help these people to feel less scared as they start to deal with the real issues confronting them and their children.

Anger

Anger is a further stage in the separation process, which can cause problems for some parents. Some degree of anger is normal at separation. It is part of the grieving process and only becomes a problem when we express it inappropriately or when, instead of diminishing with time, it continues to grow. This type of anger builds into a rage, which interferes with our capacity to think and plan in a rational way about the separation. It overwhelms us and can seriously threaten our capacity to parent cooperatively.

In Chapter 6, we noted that cultural beliefs about fault and blame at separation often support our natural anger in ways that make it even more intense. These beliefs do this by giving us permission to direct our rage at our partner. We are told that it is better to express our anger, to get it off our chest. Many people think that it is only natural at separation to shower rage on their former partner. But if we are going to parent cooperatively after separation we need to challenge these beliefs. For the most part, the inevitable result is our former partner returns the anger with interest added, reinforcing the downward spiral into a bitter and destructive relationship. Expressing anger does not always make it go away. In fact, it sometimes does the opposite. It increases it!

In order to take charge of our anger at separation, we first have to realise that much as we may want to aim it at our former partner, it is inappropriate and destructive to do so. This is the case no matter how much we think they deserve it. Many former partners who have gone down this path of anger, bitterness and destructiveness look back at it as a time of madness in their lives. They wish they had managed to control their anger. With hindsight they can see it achieved nothing, except to keep them out of control and connected to their partner in a destructive way. While they remained connected in this way, they were not able to take charge of their own life and their future as a separate person.

Many parents have found that it helps to understand where the anger is coming from, as this seems to make it more manageable. Sometimes, the answer is to do with generalised loss, the result of an accumulation of losses over a lifetime. The separation tips the balance. At other times it is connected with the specifics of the relationship, such as an affair or perceived unfairness. It could be the result of resentment at the perceived unfairness in the relationship about roles and responsibilities, or it could be a result of a belief that the decision to separate was unilateral. We discussed both of these factors in detail in Chapter 5. If we accept that feelings are created partly by the meaning we assign to them, then changing the meaning can help to manage the feelings. For instance, former partners may attach a variety of meanings to an affair. Some people see what has occurred as a reflection of their own inadequacy and this may lead to depression. Some people see an affair as a betrayal of the marriage contract and may, in consequence, feel intense rage. Others see it as an indication of the inadequacy of their partner and just feel sad. Still others may see what has happened as a comment on the quality of the relationship. They may feel sad and angry, but the feelings are probably more manageable because they are not focused on an individual.

If anger persists and, instead of diminishing, starts to grow, it is useful to monitor when and where we feel and express it. If it erupts consistently when seeing our former partner, cutting down on the interaction is often an appropriate strategy. Some parents find alternative ways of expressing their anger, such as ringing up a good friend and telling them all about it. Another alternative is taking up hard physical exercise and work out the anger that way. For other parents, anger manifests itself in a continual battle for control. One partner, or both, hook into old battles and are unable to let go and find a new way of relating. When parents realise that they are still trying to chase the unattainable and score against their former partner, not only does the anger become less but they can also move on with their lives. If overwhelming feelings of anger persist and are seriously getting in the way of being cooperative, it is wise to seek professional assistance.

Self-blame and depression

Self-blame and depression are other behaviours that get in the way of negotiating a cooperative parenting relationship. Some aspects are discussed in Chapter 6. In particular, parents can get very stuck in their guilt about the children. One of the unintended consequences of the third narrative is that people can feel disempowered and come to believe they have failed as parents. They focus only on the negative aspects of separation for their children, instead of thinking how they can help their children in a situation which, regardless of how it came about, they now have no alternative but to confront. Many parents find it very useful to talk to other people who have experienced separation and swap stories about how they have managed their feelings. Sometimes, it is trying to deal with all these issues in isolation that is the problem and it is only when parents talk with other parents that they begin to realise how disempowered they are feeling as parents. They can then begin to challenge some of these beliefs with the support of a group or counsellor.

Questions that parents have found useful to ask themselves when they have felt paralysed by guilt include:

- What sort of havoc is my guilt creating in my relationship with my children?
- Do I want this havoc to continue?
- How did I get recruited into seeing myself as a failure? What sorts of things do I think and say that keep this view of myself going?
- Are there times when I have managed to resist this view of myself?
- Are there other people I know, in the same situation as me, who have successfully challenged these ideas? Can I ask them how they have managed to do this?

When parents start asking these kinds of questions, they begin to see that they have some choice over how they view themselves. It becomes obvious that they are allowing themselves to become tyrannised by socially constructed beliefs about how they should have behaved as a partner and a parent. They also begin to see how their current way of behaving is a self-fulfilling prophecy.

Making sense of the separation

An important stage in the clearing away of the debris is the stage where we begin to create our own account or story of what happened in the relationship. To do this we assign meanings to events and interactions, as well as our own and our former partner's behaviour. Our understanding of why the separation occurred may be very different from that of our former partner. As we saw at the end of Chapter 6, children also construct their own account of their parents separation, and their understandings of why it occurred may also be radically dissimilar from that of their parents.

These accounts or stories can be distinguished from actual events or processes in the relationship. For example, if there was violence in the relationship, this is a fact. If our partner had an affair this is also a fact. But what we tell ourselves about why our partner was violent or why our partner had an affair is not a fact. It is our interpretation of their behaviour, our way of assigning meaning to the event. When we think about relationships in this way, we can see how partners in the same relationship can have very different views of what is happening in it.

It also helps us to understand how children can have very different accounts of separation from those of their parents. They too assign meaning to the event and they do this in a way that tries to make sense of their experiences. For instance, children's experience of both their parents is usually positive. They love both of them. Therefore they find it very difficult to make sense of parent's accounts when these accounts involve blame. When one parent blames the other for the separation and responds to this blame by trying to exclude the other parent from the family, the child finds this hard to tolerate. Their experience of the other parent is very different from that of the blaming parent. Their account of the separation does not involve blame so they become distressed when they hear it. They feel trapped by divided loyalties and want to continue to have a relationship with both their parents.

How we make sense of the separation can influence how we relate to our former partner after separation. If we believe our former partner is solely responsible for the separation, then this could make it difficult for us to work cooperatively with them on children's matters. Since we assign meaning to the processes or events in our relationship, this means that we have a choice about how we construct those meanings. While we can't change the fact of separation, how we understand it can have a powerful influence on our own and our children's future. We can look at how we contributed to the separation, how our former partner contributed to it and the role of external factors. Alternatively, we can look only at how our former partner contributed, thereby exempting ourselves of responsibility, or we can look only at how we contributed and exempt the other person. Some parents focus only on external factors, such as the in-laws, work or the 'other woman', and exempt both themselves and their partner from responsibility.

Let's refer back to our three narratives. If we construct our account from a second- or first-narrative perspective, we tend to focus mainly on what one person has done to the exclusion of how the other person responded or contributed to the relationship. There has to be someone or something to blame. If we are more influenced by the third narrative, which emphasises taking some degree of responsibility for our relationships, we will also focus on what we contributed to the separation. This does not mean that we will not feel angry with our partner or that we will not attribute part of the responsibility to them for the separation.

From the third-narrative perspective, rarely is a separation totally the responsibility of only one person or totally due to outside factors. Responsibility is usually taken by both partners, although there may be varying degrees of contribution. External factors are also usually involved. Yet this way of thinking about relationships is foreign to many people. For the most part, the idea that both members of the couple created the relationship is difficult to accept. Although one partner may be seen to have 'exploited' the other, for example, the person who was 'exploited' may well need to ask themselves why they allowed this exploitation to occur. Passivity can contribute to the unravelling of a relationship just as much as direct action.

Take the example of affairs. There are many different explanations for affairs. Sometimes, an affair signals that something is really wrong with the relationship and both partners need to look at how they are relating to each other. But some people will focus only on the affair, without looking at what was happening in the relationship that contributed to the affair. This does not mean that the partner who had the affair does not have to take responsibility for that action. It does mean, however, that the affair is only one factor leading to the difficulties in the relationship. Sometimes, a person has a series of affairs, which the other partner knows about. In this case, aggrieved partners need to ask themselves why they tolerated this form of behaviour. Sometimes, people take no action in the hope that the problem will go away.

As we saw in Chapter 6, partners grow apart because they want different things from the relationship. Misunderstandings escalate, contributed to by a difference in attitude between men and women and a cultural belief in unequal roles. An understanding of these factors helps former partners to make a realistic assessment of their relationship and what they each contributed to the separation.

Sometimes outside factors play a big role and it is appropriate to assign some of the responsibility to these factors. We saw how the relationship between Bill and Lilly (Chapter 4) nearly came apart because of their confused feelings about an egalitarian relationship when children came along, and also because they lacked family and social support in caring for their children. Some of these factors were outside the couple's control. The lack of a family-friendly workplace made it difficult for both of them.

But many other factors outside the relationship can play a part in unravelling relationships. For instance, there is a higher rate of separation in families where a child dies or is severely disabled. Overwhelming stress can take its toll and contribute to partners moving apart. But even here, if former partners take personal responsibility for their relationship, they will probably be able to identify points where they could have responded differently to each other and would choose to do so if a similar situation ever occurred again. When we look back at our relationships, we can often identify alternative pathways that we might have taken had we known differently at the time. Reflecting on our role in the separation helps us to learn how to handle similar situations more effectively in the future. If we allow it to, experience will teach us how to become more creative in constructing new relationships.

Some people are able to build a cooperative parenting relationship even when they continue to blame their former partner. They quarantine their feelings and refuse to let them influence how they respond to the other parent. But these people are rare. Usually, when former partners construct an account of their relationship that places most of the blame on the other, without looking at their own contribution to the separation, it influences how they relate to each other in a negative manner. They remain in the role of victim and continue to feel aggrieved.

Reflecting on why we chose that particular partner, looking at how the relationship developed and the pattern or sequence of events can be illuminating. Many people who reach this point say that they begin to feel renewed energy and start to look forward to building a new life. They may never reach the point of liking their former partner, but they will be able to tolerate them. But parents need not wait to reach this point to start to build their parenting. Once they have cleared away some of the debris and their feelings are under a degree of control, they can begin. While the parenting relationship is functioning, even at a minimal level, trust and tolerance will increase, helping to sweep away more of the debris.

First steps in building a parenting agreement

It is a common misunderstanding that continued conflict and anger in the early days after separation, or even for some time afterwards, prevents parents from parenting cooperatively. This is not the case—what really matters is how conflict and anger are handled. It is also important to realise that when things go well initially, it does not necessarily guarantee that all future difficulties have been resolved. Some couples who manage to forge a cooperative relationship in the early days after separation find that conflict arises further down the track. Conflicts over new issues, such as repartnering or one parent wanting to move to a new geographical area with the children, can present real challenges to the parenting relationship.

Inventing your own parenting agreement is an opportunity to think creatively and build a parenting relationship that will benefit all family members. All separated parents need to think through how they are going to care for their children and settle their financial affairs. If they know what researchers say about the outcomes of separation for children, parents can look at many options to create a context that will be protective of family relationships. The key is being prepared to compromise and to find ways of listening to children.

Parents have a number of choices about how they approach these tasks. Some parents manage to make their own agreements without professional help. Usually, these are couples with low levels of conflict who find it relatively easy to contain their emotions. Such individuals, just because their emotions are under control, find it easier to access information relating to family law. These couples start out with many of the resources required for building a cooperative relationship after separation.

Other parents want assistance in forming agreements about parenting and finance and choose an alternative dispute-resolution process. Couples who choose this route are often experiencing conflict and one or both find it difficult to contain their emotions. Often, one parent is further along the path of coming to terms with the separation than the other. They may find it hard to sort out the information about family law and make sense of how it applies to them. These couples vary in their resources for building an agreement. However, they choose to settle their problems without going to court.

One way of doing this is the mediation process 'in which the participants, together with the assistance of a neutral third person or persons, systematically isolate dispute issues in order to develop options, consider alternatives and reach consensual settlement that will accommodate their needs. Mediation is a process that emphasises the participants' own responsibilities for making decisions that affect their lives.'[7]

Mediation is a cooperative process. Since parents are responsible for the final outcomes, they are more likely to come to creative agreements that are suitable for them, and are more likely to keep these agreements.

Successful parenting relationships after separation are all about 'fit'—for mothers, fathers and children. Some parents fashion parenting relationships that other separated parents would not be able to tolerate. The important factor is not how these relationships are structured but whether they work for both parents and children. Parents who are flexible in building their parenting relationships and 'think outside the box' often find solutions to dilemmas that defeat other parents. They take personal responsibility for finding these solutions.

If the mediation process is working properly, parents should not feel pressured into agreeing. Nor should they feel they are giving power to someone else to make decisions about what should happen in their family (as may happen when contested issues go to judgment in the Family Court). However, some people find the mediation process very difficult and choose to sort out their agreements through other processes. These processes include more structured negotiation processes such as conciliation or they combine mediation and the use of a family law solicitor. It is important to choose a solicitor who is concerned with working cooperatively rather than taking an adversarial position.

Many parents consult a family law solicitor before mediation to gather information on their specific situation, and they use the solicitor to check the agreement once it has been negotiated. Sometimes a family law solicitor will refer parents for mediation. Many excellent child-focused family mediation services work closely with family law solicitors and can help parents to work out a process to suit specific needs.

Other couples find themselves embroiled in high levels of conflict, which they may not be able to contain in front of the children. Emotions are out of control. For these couples, working through family law solicitors who are focused on the needs of children and who are interested in finding cooperative rather than adversarial solutions may be the preferred option. This allows parents to increase their distance, and minimise their interactions. Because they do not have to face each other, they may be more capable of reaching an agreement through a solicitor that sets a basic framework for cooperation. It may be critical for these individual parents to seek professional help to manage their emotions, if they find these emotions are not easing with time. Finally, if one party refuses to negotiate or all attempts at negotiation fail, it may be appropriate to go through the Family Court. This is also appropriate in situations of violence and abuse, where it is important to ensure protection for all concerned.

Sometimes, issues about the children become entangled with issues about how to settle financial matters. Low-conflict couples often find it possible to work out financial matters for themselves. It may help to reach agreement if financial and children's issues are dealt with together, as they are often intertwined. Mediation is often appropriate in such instances. However, when there are major differences in access to financial information among the parties or where there are major differences in power between them, mediation or sorting it out without assistance may not be appropriate. Both parents have to feel that they can speak freely, without feeling intimidated or frightened, and both have to feel they have full access to the family's financial situation. Otherwise, we are not looking at a level 'playing field'.

Non-adversarial dispute resolution is promoted and supported in family law as a first priority. Both the Family Court and the Magistrates Court (where some family disputes are also heard) encourage couples to come to their own agreements about the care of children. Some couples choose to make only key aspects of their parenting arrangements legally enforceable and, in fact, many aspects are not capable of being legally enforced. They do this to provide a safety net in case the agreement fails to last. However, some couples have developed sufficient trust and confidence in their ability to negotiate with each other that they don't find it necessary to use the law to make their agreements stick.

It is important for separating couples to familiarise themselves with family law in Australia. The Family Court has produced a small booklet called the *Family Court Book*, which is an excellent source of information on the legal aspects of separation and divorce. There are websites for both the Family Court (*www.familycourt.gov.au*) and the Child Support Agency (*www.csa.gov.au*) with similar useful information. The Family Court site *(www.csa.gov.au/pubs/me.htm)*, for instance, contains a useful booklet entitled, 'Me and my kids: Parenting from a distance'. It has been written for separated parents who spend time away from their children, and among other things, aims to help parents to become more involved in their children's lives, build stronger relationships with their children and communicated effectively with the other parent about their children. Visiting *www.facs.gov.au* and looking up the Family Relationship Program Directory will give details of family mediation and counselling services, including specific services for children.

Many parents and professionals working with separating parents have found it useful to follow one very simple rule when working out a cooperative parenting agreement: the more conflict and disorder in the separation, the more need there is to negotiate a comprehensive and detailed parenting agreement, which spells out roles and rules clearly and minimises interaction between the parents, at least initially.[8] If parents remain friendly on separation, it may be possible for them to negotiate an agreement that allows for much more interaction between them. This agreement could be less formal. But even informal agreements are based on implicit rules about how former partners expect to interact with each other and how they expect to care for their children. Most parents find it useful to make the rules *explicit* because this minimises opportunities for confusion and conflict.

The next section sets out guidelines for use in the negotiating process.

Negotiation

Negotiation is a process that can be learnt and many parents find it helpful to adopt these simple guidelines, especially if they are anxious about how to handle the situation. These guidelines can be used by couples sorting out their own agreement and in a formal mediation process. Many of these guidelines draw on the work of Fisher and Ury (1981)[9] and Stone et al. (1999)[10]. The guidelines are:

1. Focus on the needs of the children.
2. Agree on the rules for conducting the conversation.
3. Make an effort to understand each other's position.
4. Identify the issues and search out as many options as possible.
5. Be prepared to compromise.
6. Make clear agreements and remain faithful to those agreements.

Item 1 sets out the purpose of the parenting relationship. Items 2 to 6 are typical of a well-functioning business relationship. What follows is a discussion of each item in turn.

Focusing on children's needs

We discuss children's needs at separation in detail in Chapter 2. Although some parents spend a great deal of time arguing over what is in their children's 'best interests', they can usually agree on two basic principles:

'1. Children benefit from maintaining the familial relationships in their life that were important and meaningful to them prior to the separation.
2. Children benefit when the relationship between their parents—whether married or divorced—is generally supportive and cooperative.'[11]

The participants' acceptance of these principles reinforces the main purpose of the parental conversation, which is to focus on their parental arrangements and the children's needs. These principles are not rigidly prescriptive but can be used as a reference point to evaluate options. They allow for very different agreements to be reached, giving parents a chance to exercise their creativity. They have the opportunity to fashion a customised agreement with a firm foundation for future extensions. If parents can look at this process as an opportunity to build something new and worthwhile, rather than a horrid necessity, there is every chance they will discover innovative ways to resolve their problems and build post-separation families that really work.

Establish rules for conducting the conversation

If there is a degree of conflict between the couple and one or both of them feel that it is likely they will be overtaken by emotion, it is useful to establish explicit rules about how they will discuss issues with each other. It seems to make a difference even if only one person sticks by these rules. They provide a buffer and the conversation is not allowed to escalate out of control, even if this means that one person brings the conversation to an end by refusing to participate in a growing conflict. Rules of this kind include:

- Focus on the present and immediate future, not the past—how are we going to parent *now*?
- Treat one another with civility and politeness.
- Focus on resolving issues rather than on personalising them.
- Do not involve the children in your disputes.
- Take time out if the discussion becomes heated or if one parent feels they may lose control.

If time out is required, ensure a time is set to resume the discussion.

If negotiating the agreement without professional help, make the meeting place neutral and public. Some parents find that venues like a coffee shop or a restaurant help them to keep the conversation focused and to avoid personalising the issues.

Try to understand the other's position

In relationships that are working well, it is not usual to have to make a constant effort to understand the other's position. There is a large area of common ground. But where there is a great deal of negativity or conflict in the relationship, the people involved have to decide consciously to make an effort to change their mindsets and listen more positively to one another. If this effort is not made, it is almost inevitable that one of the parents will conclude that, when the other parent says something with which they disagree, it is an indication of underlying bad intentions and evidence of an attempt to control or punish them. This is usually enough to ignite old arguments and, before knowing it, perhaps with no conscious intention on either part, the conversation is overtaken by conflict.

Making an effort to understand the other person's position requires each parent to decide to begin the discussion with an open mind, putting aside any views they may have that their former partner is the problem. Each parent decides to *listen* to what the other has to say, rather than immediately argue and pursue their own agenda. Each must be constantly alert to the fact that their past joint history can exert a powerful influence on how they interpret the present, making it only too easy to be dismissive of what may be a genuine attempt to create a parenting arrangement.

Some parents have said that it helps them to negotiate more positively if they list their former partner's virtues (or potential virtues) as a parent and think about the person in that light. This helps to separate parenting and partner roles. Separating each is fundamental to good outcomes for children and parents. It can also help to remember that each person is probably undergoing rapid change following separation. You cannot assume that you know the other person or that they know you anymore—they may be thinking quite differently now. So you cannot predict how the other will behave or respond in the negotiation process. You neither trust nor distrust, but proceed in the absence of trust until the new parenting relationship is established and you begin to have some trust in its operation and the other person, based on the new history.

Many parents come to realise that when they really make the effort to understand each other's position, it helps them to act in a way that puts family relationships first rather than privileging the interests of the separate adults.[12] Some researchers call this acting from an 'ethic of care' rather than an 'ethic of justice'.

Identify the issues and research the options

Listing the issues that have to be negotiated and then searching out all the available options is the most practical and perhaps the most creative side of the negotiations. Issues that usually have to be sorted out at separation include the following:

- *The basics of the cooperative parenting relationship*. How will parents be involved together in the parenting endeavour? Will they meet occasionally to discuss things or will they phone each other if there is a problem? Will they occasionally do things together with the children or will everything be done separately?

- *Practical arrangements*, such as where the children will live. How much time will they spend with each parent? How will holidays be decided and occasions such as birthdays and other family celebrations handled? Who will attend parent/teacher evenings? What decisions will be shared and what decisions will parents make individually? Some parents even include issues such as who will do the children's washing and at what time. Other parents try to agree on some essentials of parenting that they know may cause conflict in the future.
- *How can the agreements be varied?* Even when parents were caring fot their children together, there were times when plans had to be changed. It is important to stick to the agreement as this reduces confusion and ambiguity, but it is also important to realise that sometimes there will need to be flexibility for the sake of the children. One set of parents agreed to vary the agreement when the children's grandparents arrived in town unexpectedly so that the children could spend some time with them.
- *How will the agreement be reviewed* to take into account the differing needs of children and parents over time?
- *Financial arrangements for children.* Most parents consult the Child Support Agency's guidelines. However, in many situations private arrangements can be negotiated that are more tailored to the specific situation.
- *The financial agreement between the parents*, which may or may not be independent of child-support issues.

A common mistake that many parents make when negotiating is to restrict their options. They shut down their creativity and thinking skills and sometimes back themselves into a corner. Instead, this is the time to take advice from a variety of sources.

Many parents consult legal and financial advisers so that they are clear about their legal rights and responsibilities in relation to both children and finance. They may consult family counsellors and mediators so that they have information on which to base their decisions about children's care and needs.

Options for children should take into account the age of the children and the length of time between seeing their parents. It is a time to talk to friends who have been through the same issues and arrived at cooperative agreements. Friends can often provide much needed advice about the pitfalls. It is important to get as many options as possible on the table, to increase the range of innovative solutions.

Many parents talk to their children about what might work for them, revealing important information on which parents can base their decisions. Children may come up with options that parents have not considered. Giving children a voice in the process about their care arrangements also allows options to be experimented with on a more flexible basis. Different arrangements can be tried to see if they really work. Ideas on how to include children in the process are discussed in more detail later in this chapter.

If parents are in great conflict, flexibility may not be appropriate. A structured arrangement that will reduce the level of conflict is more of a priority in this situation.

Be prepared to compromise

Many couples are not familiar with the dynamic process of negotiation or the fact that compromises in the short-term often mean long-term gains. Sometimes, parents become polarised in their options for looking after the children. The only options on the table are sharing children 50/50 or a schedule that is so minimal (contact every other weekend) that one of the parents is almost wholly marginalised. This is when people feel they are backed into a corner. There are also many other options that can be explored that do not focus so much on time but on taking responsibility for looking after children's various activities, such as taking the child to a regular sporting event, music practice, or sharing an evening meal once a week. These activities are routine, regular occurrences which allow parents and children to maintain contact through doing normal things together. This is protective of relationships. Getting some other options on the table—such as contact every other weekend and one evening per week; or a pick-up from school on Friday and return to school on Monday every other weekend, plus one evening per week—can break the deadlock. When parents become polarised, it can be worth exploring how these options shape up against their agreed principles—protecting the children's relationship with both of them and not subjecting children to loyalty dilemmas. Is the proposed 50/50 arrangement being proposed on the basis of fairness to adults or is it really in the children's best interests? Is every other weekend really protective of the children's relationship with the other parent? Explaining the options can lead to getting some other options on the table.

If both parents can agree to one of these (or many alternative) compromise positions and make it work, it sets a context in which they can demonstrate to each other that they can parent together and perhaps entertain the possibility of even greater cooperation in the future.

Another area that often needs compromise is when parents have different needs about flexibility and certainty. One parent may prefer not to plan, or make only provisional plans, and keep all options open, while the other parent may be the opposite. They have very different styles of planning for the future and need to work out a compromise. Children like both predictability and certainty.

Make clear agreements

Parents run into difficulties with their agreements for a number of reasons, but mainly because agreements are not tailored to their situation. The basic rule of thumb is that the more conflict in the parents' relationship, the more specific they need to be in their agreement, and the more they need to minimise their own interaction, at least in the short term. Specific details give parents clear guidelines on how they will act in any given situation, particularly in situations where there is likely to be conflict—in essence, the parents agree to cooperate around their non-cooperation. Parents can be very detailed in these agreements because they know the issues that are going to be difficult for them to handle. Some couples agree to hand over the children at the front door to reduce their meetings with each other. They might agree to a phone call once a week to discuss any concerns about the children.

Remaining faithful to the agreements made is discussed in the next chapter.

Negotiating takes practice. If parents want to build their cooperative parenting relationship over time, these guidelines provide a foundation for helping them negotiate the many tricky situations that they will inevitably encounter at some point. If we were to look at cooperative parents who have more informal agreements and examine their behaviour towards each other, we would find that it closely resembles these guidelines. They help all types of relationships to function—in business and diplomacy, as well as in cooperative parenting after separation.

Talking with children about their ideas and concerns

We know from research that children often feel very alone and isolated during the separation process. We can minimise this distress by talking to our children about the decision to separate and by establishing a context in which children feel they can ask questions and discuss ideas. Telling children is often one of the most difficult aspects of the separation and many parents feel ill-equipped for the task. But if parents are able to tell their children and manage to avoid pitfalls like blaming the other parent, a natural part of their ongoing interaction with the children will be talking to them about the future. If the children feel they can ask more questions and parents feel that they can return to the subject with their children, then they have laid a good foundation. It takes time for parents and children to work through significant transitions.

We know that children don't want to feel pressured to take sides and we know they hate being caught up in their parents' conflicts. They don't want to hear negative things about the other parent.

Children also need to hear a clear message that their parents are ready to listen to them and hear their concerns. Having heard their concerns, children then need to know that their parents will take these into account when making final decisions.

Children vary in their ability to articulate their concerns. Younger children may have more difficulty than older children, and of course older and younger children's concerns will vary. Sometimes children need help in identifying their feelings so that they can name their concerns: 'I feel sad because I will miss living with both of you. I will worry if you are okay'. At other times, children may become paralysed by fear, as they believe that they have to take sides. It is important for both parents to emphasise to their children that their separation does not mean that the children have to take sides and that both parents are resolute in their determination to ensure that the children retain their relationship with both parents.

Some children are not able to articulate their concerns and views easily. If they feel pressured by their parents, they will clam up more. In these instances, it seems best to let children be and use opportunities as they arise to check out how they are managing. Children need to know that their parents have confidence in their ability to adapt to the change and this confidence may not be conveyed if parents become hypersensitive to children's responses or non-responses.

When parents genuinely consult with their children, they are trying to build up a picture of their child's world and what this change will mean for them. The more they know about this, the more their decisions can reflect arrangements that will help the child come to terms with the separation and cater for their needs. Children may identify a myriad of different concerns and parents need to be honest in their responses to these concerns. Children know that things are going to change—they usually want parents to be direct and discuss with them how they will change.

Children's concerns often cluster around a number of common areas. They want to know they are going to have a continuing relationship with both parents and they want to know how this will happen. Sometimes they know other children whose parents have separated and the children rarely see one parent. They might think that this is what happens in most separations. There are often concerns about the basic organisation of their life and how this will be affected—who will take them to school? Will their father still take them to cricket? Can their friends still come around to play? Can the dog come with them to see their other parent? Some children are very concerned about their parents welfare—how will their mum cope if they spend time at their dad's? Children also often want to know what will happen with events such as Christmas and birthdays. These things are important to them and although parents may not have answers, they can convey to their children that they understand their anxiety. All of this information helps parents build up a more complex picture of their child's world, giving them a much richer understanding of the impact of the separation on the child and a firmer basis for decision making.

Some children can talk with their parents about their thoughts on what type of arrangements might work for them. However, frequently children do not have enough information to help them think about these issues. In one recent study on children's views, children recognised that 'they were not in possession of the same knowledge as their parents but they wanted to be involved and have a say. They also wanted the opportunity to discuss practicalities'.[13] Certainly, definitive questions such as which parent they want to live with are likely to paralyse children, who may interpret it to mean that they have to take sides. Some parents find it useful to talk with the children about their ideas and the children to respond to these. The process of consulting with children is usually an iterative process, and one in which parents have to weigh up what they think is in the best interests of the child, with their own capacity to care for them, and with the concerns and wishes of the child. It is not a simple process and often can be one of trial and error. However, if children feel that their parents are genuine and they know that each parent will support their relationship with the other, this sets a context for the parents and children to work things out gradually and perhaps to even try out different arrangements. This can give children a sense of control over their lives.

Some parents can manage to experiment with flexibility in the early stages of separation. However, many find this difficult because it increases the time parents have to negotiate with each other and thereby increases the opportunities for hostilities. In these instances, it is probably best for parents to be open with the children and say they need definite arrangements for the time being. This sets the parameters for the children and also demonstrates to the children that they are prioritising issues at the moment—that is, it is better for everyone to have less fighting than to have flexibility. That might come with time.

When parents genuinely try to consult with their children on these issues, they may be confronted with the ambivalence of their own feelings. In their heads they know that their children love both their parents and want to be close to both. But in their hearts, they fear the changes separation might bring and what this will mean for their future relationship. One part of them wants to give the children a voice but the other fears what they might hear.

Some parents are able to acknowledge this ambivalence and not let it interfere with how they listen to their children. For others, the timing is not right and they cannot take on board what their children are saying. When parents have these difficulties, it may help to consult a child-focused mediation/counselling service, where parents can get support to help them work through these feelings.

Some parents find it hard to talk to their children about these matters at all and yet they still want to know what their children think. In these types of situations, parents may feel that they cannot control their own emotions or the conflict between them might spill over. It may also be that they are in disagreement about what the arrangements for the children should be and they fear that they will not be able to reach agreement. They might fear that this will also be evident to the children and that this could cause their children increased stress. A family mediation service has professionals trained to talk to children about these things and then convey the children's views to both parents. Hearing what the children think in a neutral environment might assist parents to come up with a creative solution.

There are some instances where talking with children is counterproductive. In these situations, parents consult with children for their own ends. They try to enlist the child's loyalty or they use the opportunity to be negative about the other parent. In these situations, talking with children is not helpful and is more stressful for the child than not talking at all. Some children do not want to be involved and will also convey this to their parents. Their wishes also need to be respected.

If parents are still not convinced about the wisdom of offering children a voice, they may like to take into account the potentially adverse effects of not consulting children who wish to be consulted. While it is important that parents feel their decision to involve their children is appropriate, some children, especially older children, may strongly resist solutions imposed by their parents. Children will appreciate and respect their parents for giving them the opportunity to have a voice and the arrangements agreed on will usually have a better chance of working than those arrived at without children's involvement.

A future voice

We know that children's needs vary and that care arrangements have to change to reflect this. There will be times when simple changes to a current arrangement will also make a vast difference. Once arrangements have been going for a while, children often have lots of creative suggestions about how to make them work better. This is because they are the ones who are really 'living with' the arrangements. They have experience of what it feels like and what works and what doesn't work. Sometimes children feel they are not seeing enough of one parent, or they do not have enough space to see their friends and do their homework. Sometimes the changeover days do not work well because of changes in school arrangements. If children feel they can talk to their parents about these things and have some capacity to vary the arrangement if required, this can have a very beneficial effect on their lives. If we give them the space and let them have a voice, children can teach us many things about how to make post-separation care arrangements work.

8

Maintaining the creative parenting relationship

In this final chapter, we look at the kinds of strategies that parents find useful in helping to maintain, reinforce and extend the co-operative parenting relationship, especially during important transition points such as repartnering.

Some useful guidelines

A few basic guidelines will help to maintain a cooperative relationship and keep it functioning smoothly. Most of them are about setting the parameters of the parenting relationship and remaining faithful to the agreement. Some are related to how cooperative parents talk to each other and conduct their relationship. The same rule of thumb—that the more conflict in the separation, the greater the need to negotiate the specific parameters of the parenting relationship—applies to the maintenance stage of the cooperative parenting relationship.

The cooperative parenting relationship can get into trouble if parents have not negotiated an agreement that fits their capacity to interact with each other without conflict. Where conflict is low, some parents manage to communicate clearly about their children and decide to share time together with them, such as some meals and school occasions. Other parents are still very angry with each other and find it better to maintain as much separateness as possible. It is important for parents to work out where their relationship falls on the friendliness–conflict spectrum, so they can avoid confusion on issues of this kind.

Wherever the parenting relationship fits on the anger–friendliness spectrum, many parents have found the following nine guidelines useful. They incorporate some of the points discussed in Chapter 3 and extend and build upon them. We cross reference to these guidelines.

Remain faithful to the agreement

Parents who remain faithful to their agreement recognise that it helps to build trust and confidence in each other as parents in their new working relationship. As more trust and confidence builds, it becomes easier to parent together and negotiate the difficult times that all parents confront with their children, whether they are parenting together or apart. It is important to ensure that the agreements negotiated are *workable*, if parents are to remain faithful to them.

There will inevitably be times when one parent doesn't get it right and contravenes the agreement. It is important for the one who gets it wrong to apologise, but it is also important for the other parent not to assume that their former partner is deliberately contravening the agreement and personalise the issue. If it happens a number of times, the agreement may need to be revised.

Keep to your agreed personal code of conduct

During the initial negotiations, parents agreed to treat each other with politeness and courtesy. It is a good idea to stick with this code. This is a way of ensuring that anger does not override parenting objectives. Observance of such a code helps to ease anxiety at changeover times for both parents and children. It also makes conversations about parenting less stressful when either parent has anxieties about their capacity to cope with the discussion without losing their temper.

Parents should also talk about how they will maintain and respect each other's privacy and add this guideline to the code of conduct. This is connected to our earlier guideline of treat the other parent as you would like to be treated yourself. Most separated cooperative parents want some personal privacy. Therefore it is important not to ask children for inappropriate details about their other parent and their life with them. This puts children in a difficult position. If they respond to inappropriate questions, they are being disloyal to the other parent. If they don't respond, they are displeasing the parent who is asking the questions. Many parents find that a useful reference point for assessing what is appropriate is for them to ask themselves if they would want the other parent asking the same questions about them. Children will talk about their experiences with their other parent, but listening and sharing these experiences with them is very different from questioning them about private or confidential issues concerning the other parent.

Focus on the present and immediate future

Unless you have reached a point with your former partner where it is possible to chat amiably about the past, it is better to focus on the immediate future, especially if you are trying to resolve present difficulties. This can be hard to do but parents find that, if they allow themselves to be seduced into focusing on the past, it will inevitably result in arguments about who was at fault over the break-up, or whose actions have contributed to some present difficulty with the children. Continue with a business-like arrangement for as long as this is needed.

Focus on your own contribution to recurring difficulties

This is a difficult guideline to follow, particularly if there is still a lot of pain about the separation. It is much easier to blame the other parent, than look at one's own behaviour and ask how it may have contributed to the problem. Many parents get stuck looking for the cause of the problem, not realising that the original cause may now be irrelevant to solving the problem.

Many difficulties in cooperative parenting are the result of escalating misunderstandings or continuing vicious cycles. When parents stand back and reflect on their difficulties, they often find that they are acting in inappropriate ways—such as blaming the other parent, second guessing their former partner's intentions, justifying their own behaviour or avoiding dealing with a situation. This behaviour may be contributing to the maintenance of the problem. Addressing our own behaviour can result in new and creative solutions.

Allow children to handle their own battles

When children complain about issues with their other parent, most parents find that it is better not to take the children's side immediately. It is important to recognise and understand that children have to develop and handle their own relationship with the other parent. When there is a legitimate issue, the most useful thing parents can do is to encourage their children to talk about it with the other parent. When parents reflect on children's complaints of this kind, they realise they would take exactly the same course of action if they were still together as a couple.

Complaints may also be a function of the children playing one parent off against the other. Although this happens when parents live together, it is more likely to occur when they live apart. Separated, it is more difficult for them to communicate with each other and they become more vulnerable to being manipulated by their children. Most parents believe it is important not to support this type of behaviour in their children.

On the other hand, it is important to distinguish between allowing children to handle their own battles with each parent and supporting them in situations where they may be exposed to danger, abuse or neglect. Parents and other involved adults must be open to the suggestion that things are going seriously wrong in the child's relationship with the other parent, such as where a parent is seriously abusing alcohol or drugs or becomes mentally ill. It is not uncommon for these problems to arise with separation. They also arise in intact families. They may signal that one parent is having a hard time coming to terms with the separation.

Another situation to be alert for is physical and sexual abuse, particularly by a new partner. Children seem to be more at risk from new partners. Sometimes repartnered parents are blinded by their attachment to a new partner and do not see that their children need protection.

Parenting across two households involves treading a fine line. It is important for parents not to undermine each other's parenting by forming a coalition with the children against the other parent. However, it is very important to protect children and for parents to be alert to when a complaint is legitimate, or when the children's behaviour has changed so dramatically that it is obvious that something is radically wrong.

Support the other parent's role as a parent by accepting each other's different parenting styles.

The fact that each parent may have a different parenting style is often a cause of conflict between cooperative parents and can derail a cooperative parenting relationship. The fights between the parents about whose style is right distresses the children and is more distressing and unsettling for them than any parenting differences. It is often a slow and difficult process for parents to recognise that different parenting experiences can actually be positive experiences for children. Children can cope with and adjust to different rules in each household. More often it is the parents who have difficulty adjusting and they need to reflect on whether the battles signify that they are still continuing the relationship battles by trying to control each other's behaviour.

Sometimes one parent undermines the other by commenting negatively on their parenting and encouraging children to break the rules. Many parents in this situation address the behaviour directly by raising it with the other parent and requesting the undermining stop.

If possible, build a parenting coalition

When children experience real difficulties, many parents find it easy to slip into blaming each other rather than looking at what they can do together to deal with the situation. Some parents manage to build a parenting coalition where they both agree on what needs to be done to resolve the problem and both agree to support the other's actions in their relationship with the child. This is particularly important during adolescence, when children's behaviour can be challenging and worrying for parents. In fact, a powerful motivator for many parents of younger, more compliant children to work more cooperatively is to think about how they will cope alone with rebellious adolescents.

Allow others to be themselves

This is a difficult step for many parents but once taken often has a very positive effect on the cooperative parenting relationship. Many parents spend time trying to get the other parent to change, not realising this is a futile effort. If you couldn't change them when you lived with them, it's hardly likely that you will succeed now you don't! If one parent is chronically late, for example, and this has always been the pattern, it is unlikely that they will change now. The best solution is probably just to accept that this is likely to happen and *plan around it*.

Allow children to have access to their other parent

It is important to allow children contact with their other parent when they change households or are on a contact visit. This can be as simple as allowing them to phone and talk about what they are doing. At other times, children may need to organise some aspect of their lives for which they rely on the other parent. Permitting this type of access to their other parent gives a child a sense of control over their life, and they can tell Mum or Dad important things as they arise. This can be very important and reassuring to children and ease their anxieties at leaving the other parent.

Some parents place restrictions on their children's contact with the other parent, believing that the contact somehow detracts from their relationship with the children. However, it is the experience of many parents that, if they allow their child to contact the other parent when the child requests this, this need for contact with the other parent stabilises with time.

Review any agreements

Just when the arrangements seem to be working well, something intervenes that means the agreement has to be adjusted. This may be a change to parent's working hours, a change to school schedules, or children growing older and wanting a different type of arrangement. One parent may re-partner and need to revise the agreement. It is crucial that parents recognise that an agreement cannot be for ever but will need adjusting from time to time.

Typical flashpoints in cooperative parenting

Children who find changeovers difficult

Children differ in how easy or difficult they find changeovers (i.e. the process of moving) between parents and places. When children find them difficult, some parents interpret this to mean that the children are unhappy with the parenting arrangements. This is not necessarily so. It is not unusual for some children to find changeovers difficult in their own right, especially in the beginning. Just as a child leaving to spend time with his father is a reminder of the separation for his mother, so it may be a reminder of the separation for the child. As well as this, the child has to deal with a more immediate loss[1]—that of leaving one parent to go to another. The younger the child, the more likely it is that they will experience some attachment anxiety, especially if they are under four years of age. Developmentally, they cannot keep in their mind an image of the absent parent.[2] Younger children's concept of time is also less well developed, so they may be confused about when they will see the other parent again.

Children's reactions vary—some become 'clingy'; some need time to adjust; some throw tantrums; some are fine the moment the transition is made; others are cranky and irritable for a while. On the other hand, some children handle changeovers very well from a young age, indicating that they are capable of making multiple attachments. Things are different for different children and problems on this score are not necessarily caused by problems in the cooperative parenting relationship.

The recognition that difficulties in changeovers are normal for some children, especially in the beginning, can help parents to calm down and make decisions about how to handle them. The flashpoint often comes because parents blame each other. They see it as being caused by the way the other parent is responding to the child. They may use the difficulties as a reason not to let the child go, or to try to change the arrangements without giving the agreement a fair chance to work. Here are some of the things that parents have found helpful when children have difficulties with changeovers:

- *Normalise the changeovers as much as possible.* Make them into stable routines and encourage children to keep track of them.
- *Try not to make changeovers hard work for children.* If they have to pack half their room and carry too many things between houses, the process becomes too difficult. Children often complain about this.
- *Check whether you, as parents, are conveying your own anxieties* about the changeover to the children. Some children worry about leaving a parent alone. They pick up on their parent's insecurities. Sometimes, children's difficulties are a sign of parental anxiety.
- *Make sure the changeover is not a time of conflict and argument between parents.* Some children dread changeovers because they are confronted with the reality of their divided loyalties. The only way for them to cope is to be hyperactive, aggressive or 'clingy'. If parents find they can't stop fighting at changeover time or making negative comments, they need to find a different way to handle changeovers, such as being picked up from school or by using a contact centre.

  It makes sense that the more relaxed the parents are with the changeover, the more relaxed the children will be. Some parents find that the time immediately after the children have left is difficult to handle; it helps if they have planned some activity, such as seeing friends.
- *Try not to assume that it is the other parent's fault.* If the difficulties continue, see if you can discuss how you might handle it together. Many parents are surprised to find that their child is having a general difficulty with changeovers—not just leaving them. If the difficulties continue, seek professional help.

A professional might be able to build a picture of the child's world and find out what is happening for them. Children may not be able to tell their parents those things.

Negotiating major changes

Sometimes, parents have to renegotiate their agreements and make major amendments to them. This is often a consequence of one parent having to relocate to another area, making the current agreement redundant. This can become a major flashpoint, pushing parents back into serious dispute. If handled creatively, however, parents can often find solutions which, while not ideal, are better than one parent withdrawing totally from their children's life. For the most part, parents who are working cooperatively to parent their children try to avoid this type of situation precisely because it can be so difficult to negotiate.

Cooperative parenting is obviously easier if the parents live a manageable distance from each other but, sometimes, they have no choice or the choices are limited. Many people are required to move for their work; some parents may be required to move to find work so that they can continue to pay much needed child support. Sometimes, a move happens because one of the parents marries or repartners. This can complicate the situation even further.

So how can parents negotiate this issue successfully without getting caught up in unnecessary conflict? One way that some parents have found useful is to go back to the negotiating table, using the guidelines described at the beginning of Chapter 7. To achieve success, it is important that both parents try to put themselves in the other person's position. Otherwise, the temptation will be for one or, indeed, both parents to think that the other is manipulating the situation to alter the terms of the existing parenting agreement.

If the cooperative parenting relationship has been working well up to now, there are likely to be sufficient resources—such as trust, good communication and a flexible and creative approach—to define this issue as a family problem, not just as the problem of the parent who has to move. The family, including the children, can then look at options that will safeguard the parent's relationship with the children and also meet the needs of the children, as far as this is possible. Children seem to be really good at thinking up novel solutions to problems that perplex their parents, if they are given the chance.

Negotiating a financial settlement

Many parents negotiate parenting agreements and financial agreements together, but many parents also negotiate them separately. Often, the process of negotiating a financial agreement, whether together or through solicitors, creates real conflicts and stresses for the parenting relationship. Issues of fairness are brought to the fore and old issues in the relationship may be rekindled, particularly if money has always been a point of conflict.

Two kinds of issues are common. The first is the belief that, if one partner has earned more during the relationship, they are entitled to a greater share of the money and assets. The second is giving in to the temptation to use contact with the children as a lever in order to get a better deal. Another frequent difficulty is where one parent tries to use the terms of the financial settlement to punish the other parent for what is seen as their fault in bringing about the separation in the first place.

Parents need to be aware of the damage that these tactics and the conflicts they produce are likely to do to the cooperative parenting relationship and try to act in a way that safeguards the relationship. This means coming to terms with the fact that separating is an expensive business and that it is inescapable that everybody will be worse off financially. This is the inevitable outcome of dividing up joint property. It also means recognising that compromise is the way ahead and the most likely way in which all concerned will feel there has been a fair settlement.

However, the reality is that many people do seek to maximise their own interests. It also happens that some parents deliberately try to exploit their former partner financially. When this happens, some parents feel they are faced with a choice of giving in to save the relationship with the children or fighting to get a fair share and damaging the relationship with the children. Former partners, of course, often differ about what is fair.

Where there are differences about what is fair or where one partner is less cooperative than the other, it is often difficult to arrive at a solution that safeguards the cooperative relationship. Most people in this situation seem to recognise at some point that, in order to establish a viable parenting relationship, it may be necessary to give up some quite vital interests. The hope is that, over time, the other parent will come to see that an unfair settlement damages the relationship and, therefore, ultimately, the interests of the children. When one parent offers a compromise and refuses to engage in a continuing battle over the financial settlement, this can shift the dynamics and assist in establishing more reasonable negotiations. However, it is often very difficult to be the first one to offer this compromise.

Some partners who disagree radically on issues concerning the financial settlement aim to keep their financial dispute separate from their parenting. This demonstrates a strong capacity to prioritise what is important and to accept that not everything in the garden can be rosy. They may give the financial settlement over to their solicitors and agree to disagree. However, this is an exceptionally difficult path to tread and it takes a great deal of maturity not to allow such differences to interfere with the parenting relationship.

New partners and cooperative parenting

Many parents repartner at some stage after separation and divorce. Although most experience this as a time of joy and hope, it is potentially also a time when the cooperative parenting relationship faces major disruption. Repartnering is an important transition point that touches the lives of everybody involved in the new family unit, as well as affecting the parenting of the former partner most immediately concerned. The new partner may also bring children to the new family. The challenge is to create a new family without compromising the cooperative parenting relationship in the existing one. However, because it is a time of change, it is inevitable that the cooperative parenting relationship will have to adapt to accommodate these changes. Once again it is time for parents to think creatively about how they will handle this transition.

In what follows, we look at repartnering from the point of view of how it may affect the cooperative parenting relationship and the children's relationships with both parents. While cooperative parenting after separation is essentially about how former partners work together to bring up their children, the concept can also be extended to include new partners and possibly new children, as they become part of the new family.

The new family

When one parent decides to repartner, adults and children all participate in creating a new family unit. Some, if not all, of the children will also live and participate in another family unit with their other parent. This other family may include other steprelations. The adults and children involved may have similar views and feelings about the new family and what it means for them or they may hold very disparate views. The former partner will also have views on the new family, which may or may not be supportive of its formation. If the new partner has children, these children will be trying to find their place in the new family. They may live with the family full-time or part-time, or they may visit occasionally and for varying lengths of time. If the new partner does have children from a previous relationship, there may exist a cooperative parenting relationship with his or her former partner; but there could be conflict between them or the former partner may no longer be involved with the family.

There are many different ways in which new or second families can be organised and there is potential for a myriad different relationships. It is this complexity that gives them their special character and frequently makes them very rich places for children during their formative years. If they work well, children have a variety of role models, and they learn to negotiate complexity. On the other hand, this complexity can be their drawback and make it difficult for family members to cope successfully.

When parents decide to form a new relationship, they usually do so with much hope and expectation for its future. Most people do not wish to go through another separation. The new couple usually bring large amounts of energy, dedication and enthusiasm to the new family, as they really want it to work. However, unlike most first marriages or relationships, this time round there are already many people involved in the couple's relationship from the beginning. This makes relationships in second families very different from first-family relationships. If the new couple are aware of these differences and have a map in their head of what they might expect, this will be a positive help to them in establishing the new family and avoiding common pitfalls. Many of the initial difficulties experienced by second families result from the couple expecting the new family to be like their old family. In what follows, we discuss some of the major differences between first and second families.

Being a parent before becoming a partner

In a stepfamily, one or both partners are already parents before they become partners. They have other relationship responsibilities, which demand their time and dedication and predate their present relationship. This can lead to one partner feeling excluded when their partner is involved with his or her own children, or talking to the other parent about parenting matters. There is usually less time and opportunity to nurture the new adult relationship because of these other relationship responsibilities.

Yet, as we shall see, the adult relationship is the lynch-pin on which most stepfamilies function.[3] If the new partners are not able to build a strong relationship, one that can resist challenges from the children, then not only the relationship but also the new family will fall apart. The new partners need to have a clear idea about appropriate step-parenting roles and to be realistic in their expectations of children's behaviour.

Learning to be a step-parent

At the same time as the partners are building their own relationship, one or maybe both of them are also having to learn how to be a step-parent. This is true whether the new partners are married or cohabiting. The step-parent role can be very demanding, particularly if the children are less than supportive of the new family. The situation is made even more complicated by the fact that our models for step-parenting behaviour are a little outdated in the context of cooperative parenting arrangements. Our ideas about stepfamilies come mainly from the first and second narratives that we looked at and fit poorly with the cooperative parenting reality of both parents remaining involved with parenting.

In traditional models, the step-parent tends to take on a principal parenting role, replacing the former parent who has either died or has little contact with the children as the result of a traditional separation and divorce. A principal parenting role is one where the step-parent takes on all the traditional functions of a biological parent and assumes an authority position over the child. It is much more common when children are young or the biological parent is no longer around.

Many of today's stepfamilies differ from first- and second-narrative families because the children still have two involved parents. This is the type of stepfamily we are talking about here, because we are looking at how the formation of a second family, or stepfamily, can affect the cooperative parenting relationship of the previous partners. But many step-parents adopt a traditional step-parent model, because that is the model that they know most about. The Brady Bunch has a lot to answer for! As a result, many new step-parents and often their partners have unrealistic expectations of their roles and the kinds of behaviour their children are likely to exhibit.

In a stepfamily where the previous partners have a cooperative parenting relationship, step-parents usually have to work out a role that is not a principal parenting role, as the child or children already have two involved parents. Modern step-parenting is a new phenomenon for which we have few rules and maps from the past. New partners have to be imaginative and creative in how they organise their roles in the family and in relation to the children's other parent. With time this step-parent role may become very important and take on many aspects of a principal parent role, but it will never replace the children's other parent.

The step-parent role benefits from being clearly negotiated between the new partners, with each partner's expectations made clear. It is helpful for new partners to think about developing their own parenting plan in which they are clear about how they will support each other, what they expect from each other, how conflict will be handled and the new partner's role in relation to the children's other parent.

The role a step-parent takes also depends on the age of the children. If children are in their teens, for example, the more successful strategy is usually to adopt the role of a friend. If children are younger, the step-parent may take more of a parental role but it is usually more successful if this role is of a secondary nature, at least at the beginning of the relationship. This usually means acknowledging very clearly to the children that the step-parent is not their biological parent and does not expect to replace that parent. It also means making it clear to the children that the step-parent will support the children's relationship with both their parents.

Initially, as a secondary parent, the step-parent does not usually move into a position of authority with the children. The natural parent retains this position. However, with time, as the relationship between step-parent and stepchildren grows, step-parents will assume more authority and can become very significant figures in their stepchildren's lives. Major decisions about the children's lives, such as where they attend school and their religious education, will ultimately remain the province of the natural parents.

Children adjusting to new roles

A child choosing to become a member of a stepfamily happens only rarely. The adults choose each other as partners but children do not choose the new partner as a parent. Children may be very reluctant members of the new family. The fact that children in second families frequently have another family in which they also live can give them a choice or an illusion of choice, to opt out of the new family. Their reluctance may moderate the adults' hope for the new family from an early stage.

Just as when parents separate, children and adults are often in different frames of mind when parents repartner. When they separate, many parents are already looking forward with hope to a new life, but their children, far from sharing such feelings, often want the parents to get back together. Similarly, when parents repartner, the parents are full of hope but many children do not want any more change and prefer to keep the situation as it is.

Children have to adjust to new roles and new hierarchies in the family. The eldest child may suddenly find that he or she is no longer the eldest, but has been supplanted by an older stepbrother or stepsister, with whom it is necessary to negotiate a sibling role. Children also have to adjust to having a new parent, with whom their mother or father is having an intimate relationship. This can lead to children feeling excluded and working hard to ensure that the new couple have little time together. The child's experience of the new family may be very different from their parent's experience. This can be hard for parents to understand.

Diffuse family boundaries

The boundaries in a second family are not as clear as in first families. Until the couple has children of their own, all the children are likely to be members of two households, but these two households may not necessarily be the same two. If there are two sets of children, they will be members of different households. As a result parents have to negotiate care responsibilities across two and sometimes three households. Because children move families, there is more chance of comparison across families. This often leads to issues of fairness among the children, because the way of judging these matters differs across households.

The new couple or new partner may also feel that too many people are involved in their family. They feel they can never make decisions about the children without consulting others. This can be very frustrating and cause conflict between the new couple.

Who is in the family?

Stepfamilies often struggle with the issue of who is in the family. While the new partners may define all their joint children as being part of the family, children who have no biological ties to each other often see it differently, at least initially. It takes time for stepbrothers and stepsisters to include each other as members of the same family. This is more often the case when some children have only occasional contact with their non-resident parent or the home is not seen as their primary residence. It often seems easier to define people as members of a family if everyone lives in the same house. The same issue applies to step-grandparents and other family members. This lack of unanimity about who is in the family can cause tension and conflict in the new family for some time.

Different family members have different ideas about who is in this family.

How the family deals with the complexity of all these differences will either bolster or undermine the cooperative parenting relationship, as well as the repartnering parent's relationship with his or her children. It is the experience of many of these new families that the issues that dominate the first couple of years usually concern members of the family feeling they are not being treated fairly, feeling excluded, or as though their loyalties are constantly divided. It will become more obvious why this is the case as we discuss some of the common challenges and transition points for second families. It is also obvious, given the complexity of stepfamilies, that everyone involved will benefit if individuals can be flexible in their responses to the inevitable challenges in putting the family together.

The decision to repartner

The decision to repartner is a difficult one for many parents. The bad press given to stepfamilies makes many parents worry about how their children will be affected and whether they are doing the right thing. Parents may anguish over the decision. Some parents decide not to live with their new partner because the new relationship seems too complex for them to deal with. Some put off living together until the children are older, while others live together part-time and have minimal interaction with each other's children.

No one can make this decision but the people involved. However, looking at how they might handle some of the issues and demands of a second family can help in the decision-making process. These include such issues as:

- finances;
- space requirements for children;

- relationships with former partners;
- expectations of each other on parenting issues;
- children's responses to the new partner;
- children's respones to the idea of their parent being in a new relationship.

Discussion of these issues can definitely help couples to assess how realistic a decision to live together or marry is at this point.

Reaction of the other parent

Once the decision to re-partner has been made, most parents find that it is very important to let the other parent know what is happening well in advance and to reassure them of their continued intention to parent cooperatively. The other parent may have significant fears, including the fear that the new partner will not support the idea of persisting with the cooperative parenting relationship. This is not surprising—one stereotypical story in our culture consists of the new partner insisting that their partner cease all interaction with the 'ex'. The parent who is not re-partnering may also fear that the new partner will try to take over their parent role. This fear is reinforced by another stereotypical story where the new partner competes with the former partner to prove that they can do better than the 'ex'.

The other parent may also be very concerned about how caring and loving the new step-parent will be with the children. In the case of former partners who are relatively friendly, meeting the new partner may alleviate these fears. With former partners who are not so friendly, the other parent may only be reassured with time and by seeing how the children respond to their new step-parent.

A decision to repartner may also raise old issues for the other parent, especially if they have not quite come to terms with the separation. If the announcement takes them by surprise or they find out through the children, they may find it difficult to handle their emotions. It also often happens that children, in the short term and sometimes even in the long term, are disturbed by a parent's decision to repartner. The parent who is repartnering will need the other parent's support to help the children through their reactions and to be understanding and patient if the children 'act up'.

For all these reasons, it is important to look after the cooperative parenting relationship by keeping the other parent well informed and giving them some time to digest the decision.

Children's reactions to the decision

The reactions of children to the decision to repartner are extremely varied and depend on a number of factors. Some children take it in their stride and look forward to the new situation, while others react very negatively. Most parents have found that it works better to introduce a new partner slowly and for new partners to take their cues from the children about how slowly or quickly the relationship develops.

Children seem to accept the idea of a permanent relationship if they have had time to get to know the new partner and form a reasonable relationship. Children will usually also accept a new partner more easily if they have come to terms with their parents' separation and the fact that their parents will not get back together. However, this is no guarantee of acceptance, as children may find they really enjoy the exclusive relationship they have had with their parent since the separation and do not want to share it with another person. Children's reactions also vary according to their age—teenagers may be far less interested in being part of a new family than younger children, because they are preparing to become independent adults themselves.

Many parents have to struggle with the fact that their children are less than enthusiastic, even when they appear to like the new partner. Sometimes children feel very ambivalent. They may have formed an attachment to the new partner, but when the formal decision is made their loyalty to their natural parents is activated. A child may also be concerned for their other parent, who may not have repartnered. The child might need to be reassured by the other parent that they can manage the idea of the new partner. Some children still hold on to the hope that their parents might get back together and the new partner is a reminder that this is unlikely to happen. Sometimes, children are just frightened of change and wonder where they will fit in this new family.

While many parents take note of their children's wishes in this situation, it is important to be clear that the decision to repartner is the adult's decision, just as the decision to separate was. However, in making this decision many parents consider their children by ensuring that the new partner shares similar expectations of parenting and is aware that, for the relationship to work, the family as a whole has to work. As usual, the more the repartnering parent communicates with the children, includes them in the plans, allows them to have some control over issues that are important to them, listens to their concerns and helps them find their place in the new family, the more likely it is that the children will cope with this transition.

Extended family reactions

Other extended family members can play an important role in helping to establish the new family. Just as their initial support for a cooperative parenting relationship between the former partners provided a strong message of positive support for the children, so too their support for the new partners is important in helping children come to terms with the new situation. Grandparents, in particular, can often help by listening to children and helping them see the positive aspects of the situation.

Sometimes, other extended family members are concerned that their relationships will change when a new partner enters the family. It is important for the new partner to be supportive of their relationships.

Common difficulties for the new family

Second families experience a number of common difficulties, but they vary in intensity and in the time it takes to resolve them. Research suggests that it takes a couple of years for second families to settle down[4] and feel that they have finally become a unit in their own right. Knowing what issues one may encounter can assist in their early resolution. A recent British study found that most step-parents were happy in their relationships. However, when compared with first families, a larger minority said they were unhappy.[5]

The central issue that most stepfamilies have to confront is how to reach some kind of agreement on how the family will function—who will take what roles and how they will relate to each other? Often parents believe that they can impose their views on these matters on the children but this usually doesn't work. With regard to creating a new family, children are often far less adaptable and flexible than their parents, who have to be the ones to take the lead in finding imaginative solutions.

However, it is important not to be overly pessimistic and focus only on the difficulties, as this may become a self-fulfilling prophecy. It is easy in second families for parents to get caught up in sorting out difficulties and feeling responsible for everyone's happiness. Because children do not *choose* to be in a second family, parents and new partners often feel guilty and let their feelings of responsibility overwhelm them to the detriment of looking after their own relationship.

One trap that parents fall into is to attribute all the children's difficulties to being in a stepfamily. This gives children a constant excuse to behave badly and makes it unnecessary for them to take responsibility for their own behaviour. Understanding the problems and frustrations children experience under such circumstances is one thing—condoning bad behaviour is quite another. Many parents say that an important turning point for them is the realisation that they cannot make it perfect for their children and that some difficulties just have to be lived with. Children have to live with difficulties in first families too. This realisation frees the new parents to enjoy the good times and reinforce the positive aspects of the new family.

Challenges for the new couple

One major task for the new couple is to establish a family situation that allows their relationship to develop, as well as nurturing other relationships in the family. Second families, like first families, seem to flourish when the adult couple form a strong bond and feel secure in their relationship. We discussed in Chapter 2 how the quality of the couple relationship is pivotal to the quality of life of everyone in an intact or first family. This applies just as much to second families. If the couple are constantly in conflict or unhappy with each other, the family will not thrive.

It is often hard for a new couple to nurture and develop their relationship in a stepfamily because, unlike in first families, they are often confronted with handling difficult children's issues from the very beginning of their relationship. This can be a severe test of their commitment. The couple have to sort out the issues that all new couples have to sort out together—such as who will take what role and how they will handle conflict—only they have to do so in the context of an established family that is making other demands.

Because being in a second family makes more demands on the couple relationship, the new couple need to support each other and not let the children's issues dominate their relationship. This is hard to achieve because the children, feeling insecure with all the changes, redouble their efforts to get the adults to focus on them, especially in the early stages of the new couple relationship. Some children will challenge the new relationship. They are resentful and oppositional, and they let their parents know this. These reactions need to be anticipated. Parents can listen to their children's feelings and help them to deal with them, but it is counterproductive for children to learn that their behaviour can disrupt their parent's relationship. It is not helpful for children to discover that they are more powerful than their parents. Once again, adopting the authoritative style of parenting can bring more positive results.

Sometimes, new partners find it hard to allow themselves the time as a couple to build their relationship, especially if the children are reacting negatively. Parents feel guilty because they believe the children think that he or she is putting the new partner before the children. If both new partners have children, they may often feel torn between each other and the children. If the new stepparent has no children, he or she is likely to feel that the couple relationship always comes second to the parent/child relationship.

If the new couple give in to this guilt or the children's behaviour, they are reinforcing the cause of the problem—which is the children's belief (and sometimes that of the new partner) that one family relationship means more than another. While this belief persists, everyone will compete for time and attention. The value of a relationship comes to be measured by the amount of time given to it.

One of the issues that nearly everybody in a stepfamily has to come to terms with at some stage is that time spent with one person in the family does not detract from how they feel about other family members. There is enough affection and love for everyone. If parents feel they are giving enough time and attention to their children, including some special time alone with them to ease the transition, it becomes critically important for the children to learn that adults need time together too. If the adults in the new family feel supported by each other and are able to form a cohesive couple, the existence of this strong relationship will help them to ride out the inevitable challenges to the new family from the children. This will benefit everyone in the family.

If there are two sets of children in the new family, they are likely to spend some time reacting to each other and sorting out their place. The new couple should be alert to the fact that each child may be feeling divided loyalties and these divided loyalties can cause conflict between them.

It is not unusual for new partners to feel that the other acts unfairly in relation to their stepchildren while always taking the side of their own children. New second-family parents can easily slip into 'my children and your children' conversations and, of course, once the children see the parents fighting, their behaviour is reinforced. It is very important in these early days to ease the situation and bring down the emotional barometer by acknowledging the children's feelings and reassuring them that they are loved. It also helps if the couple can keep calm themselves and not allow the children's fighting to come between them.

There are many dilemmas for the new couple initially in how they define their relationship to the children, both publicly and privately. The 'my children, your children conversation' is frequently negative and hostile and it may be a sign that the children are managing to come between the new couple. However, some stepfamily parents also find it difficult to know how to describe their family even when things are going well. Some tentativeness in this area is inevitable at first until both partners feel sufficient familiarity to talk about 'our children'. But there is a difficulty here too, because the step-parent isn't the principal parent and it could be seen as inappropriate to say 'my children', especially by the other parent of the children. This is one example among many where our language is deficient.

As a result, people are left feeling vaguely uncomfortable with how they describe their relationships, and what they say is open to misinterpretation.

It is also very important for the new couple to establish their expectations of themselves as parents and step-parents. If either partner has unrealistic expectations of the step-parenting role, it will set up the new family for failure. If either partner feels they have failed, they may become angry and direct the anger towards the other person because their partner has been unable to meet their expectations. It is very unrealistic to expect a new partner to take on a principal parenting role, at least in the beginning, and it is also unrealistic to expect step-parents and stepchildren to love each other straight away. Because the new partners love each other, they sometimes want other members of the new family to do so too. But, as we have seen, stepfamilies are different and children do not choose their new step-parent and step-siblings. Love often does develop with time, as respect and trust grow, but it rarely happens immediately. If the new partners do not expect their children to love everyone in the family immediately, it can take an enormous amount of pressure off everyone.

The cooperative parenting relationship may go a bit awry at this time and the new couple may feel that unfair demands are being made on them by previous partners. Sometimes, the new partner will feel that a former partner is interfering in the new family, and this may well be the case. However, what the new partner takes as interference may be a quite normal part of the cooperative parenting relationship.

If the new couple experience the behaviour of former partners differently and have diverse interpretations of their motives, they will need to find a way of renegotiating the boundaries in the new family. However, the new partner needs to be clear that the motivation for their behaviour is not a wish to exclude the children's other parent from performing their legitimate role.

When children have trouble accepting a new partner

Some children react by rejecting the new partner. This may resolve itself fairly quickly but sometimes it persists, causing chronic stress in the family, the couple relationship and sometimes in the cooperative parenting relationship. Children often become insecure when one or both of their parents repartner. They demand more of their parent's time and attention, at the same time rejecting the new partner. The child may see the new partner as a competitor. If the new partner has children too, it is possible that they will also react this way. Emotions in the family may seem to be constantly running on high.

It takes time for children to accept the new partner and they may display their non-acceptance in a number of ways. They may be rude or disobedient, or ignore the step-parent, excluding them from family activities. They may try to monopolise their parent's attention. They may start to 'act up', getting into trouble at school. In fact, you can expect many of the same behavioural responses that children display on separation. The biological parent may well feel torn between the new partner and the child. The step-parent will find it hard to put up with the child's behaviour and may feel hurt and excluded.

It is important to stress that relationships take time to develop and children in this situation need reassurance that the parent loves and cares for them. It is also crucial that the step-parent does not try to take on a parental role in these circumstances but concentrates on developing a relationship with the child at whatever level is possible. The natural parent needs to assume the authority role.

It is also helpful to try to work out what is going on with the child who finds it hard to accept the new partner. It could be that they believe they are betraying the other parent, or that the parents might get back together again. If this is the case, just listening to the child's feelings and acknowledging them often helps. However, most parents have found that it is important to set limits on their child's behaviour towards the new partner. They make it clear that no one expects the child to love the new partner, but it is expected that everybody will maintain certain standards of conduct towards one another. The natural parent needs to enforce these standards.

The new partner feels on the outside

When a child does not accept a new partner, the new partner often struggles with feelings of exclusion. Troubles with a stepchild may bring on these feelings, but so can positive or happy times in the family from which the step-parent feels excluded.[6] The difficulty is that the couple are trying to establish an intimate adult relationship at the same time as they are trying to nurture their parental relationships. Intimacy involves sharing important experiences and parenting is one of these experiences. In first families, the couple share this experience together. New partners, however, are often excluded from sharing their partner's parenting experience simply because they have no shared history in this area. The new partner cannot share past experiences and may be prevented by the children, at least initially, from sharing in present experiences.

Step-parents may find themselves on the outside of many positive family experiences. Many new partners say they experience feelings of resentment and jealousy towards their stepchildren because they feel excluded. Most of them are astounded by this and feel angry and disappointed in themselves for feeling this way. Although they can think rationally about it, emotions often overwhelm them.

It also helps to build step-parenting relationships if step-parents openly support their stepchildren's relationship with the other natural parent. This helps to ease children's anxiety about disloyalty to their absent parent. It also helps if the step-parent understands the child's need, at least in the early stages, for separate time with their natural parent.

Many stepchildren will openly resent and struggle against a step-parent who tries to take on a principal parenting role in the early stages of the new family. This may change later on, when children often appreciate having a third adult who will do things with them that their natural parents may resist doing. Sometimes, stepchildren reach the stage where they can appreciate the qualities of their step-parent without having to make a comparison with their natural parents. The step-parent becomes as natural—as much part of the furniture—as their natural parents. In fact, once a stepfamily is working well, children can benefit enormously from having a third parent.

Dealing with children's battles

Many children in second families complain that they are treated unfairly. When there are two sets of children they frequently struggle to establish a new pecking order. Some children experience issues of fairness when it comes to sharing their parents. They may feel that the addition of another child to the family has taken their parent away from them or stops them from having special time with their parent. They may find it difficult to adjust to children who 'visit' rather than live in the house, not seeing them as members of the family. They may also think that such children are privileged if they are treated differently. However, the child who is moving between households may feel equally excluded.

Very often, the two sets of children in the new family will have completely different access to money and toys, simply because they come from different families. The constant comparison can create animosity between children who feel that other members of the family are more privileged. All these issues are part of the adjustments that have to be made in stepfamilies, and which new couples have to learn to handle.

It is important for partners to stress to the children that, while they understand that all the children may not get along, they will not allow mayhem to reign. An expectation from parents of politeness, civility and some degree of tolerance on the part of everyone is important. This establishes a context for relationships to grow and develop in a way that is helpful for everyone.

Another strategy that some parents find useful is to make the rules of the house explicit and ensure that all the children, no matter what time they spend in the house, participate in making these rules. This gives children some control over their environment and emphasises that all children are part of the family. It also involves them in solving the central challenge for all new stepfamilies—how the family is going to function. Children who are involved in this way will feel they have more ownership of the decisions and are more likely to honour them.

Arguments between children are often about territory and many parents find that it helps if all family members have a place that is their own in the house. If children who have not previously shared a room are suddenly forced to start sharing, it underscores their loss and increases territorial fights. Having their own private space also provides a retreat for each member of the family when they feel the need for privacy. This helps to bring down the emotional temperature—it seems to reinforce the idea that it is okay to have personal boundaries and to take closeness at their own pace.

However, resources are often scarce and the new partners are not able to afford housing that offers such space opportunities. Many parents do the best they can and cordon off space, perhaps using a bookcase as a room divider, so that the child feels there is somewhere they can call their own.

The cooperative parenting relationship

Somewhere, among all these challenges, the repartnering parent has to look after the cooperative parenting relationship. During the transition to a new family, children will often complain about their parent's new partner and their repartnered parent's behaviour to their other parent, expecting the other parent to side with them. It could be very tempting for the other parent to do just that, particularly if they have not yet come to terms with the separation and there are lingering feelings of anger and revenge that might be activated by the situation. However, it is important for the other parent to realise that forming an alliance with the children against the step-parent will only intensify their children's distress and prolong a difficult situation.

At this stage, it is important for cooperative parents to go back to their ground rules and try to resolve the difficulties using the guidelines outlined in Chapter 7. It seems to help if the children's other parent acknowledges the children's feelings, but does not engage in supporting the children against the step-parent or parent. The other parent might talk with the children and brainstorm constructive ways of handling the issues in the other household, thereby encouraging children to sort out their own problems for themselves. If the children seem very disturbed, the former partner could ask their other parent to discuss with them what is happening to see if there is any way in which they can assist. This is very different from taking the children's side. It represents a creative solution to supporting children through this new transition.

It also seems to help if the repartnering parent acknowledges to the children's other parent that there are difficulties and accepts that this might have an impact in the other parent's household. Many cooperative parents even though they work together to parent their children, will not have a sufficiently good relationship to do this. However, where the relationship between former partners is friendly, and the new partner supports their cooperative parenting relationship, all the adults in a parenting relationship with the children may form a parenting coalition.

A parenting coalition is simply an agreement to act in certain ways with the children. It is particularly useful when children are having a hard time dealing with change. Parenting coalitions also work to build trust between a new partner and a former partner, helping to ensure not only that tensions and conflicts between households are reduced but also that positive, supportive relationships are built that help families to function well. Many parents are surprised when they first hear about parenting coalitions and see them as a utopian ideal. However, it is the reality that many separated couples are successful in building such coalitions.

Both the former partner and the new partner may initially feel insecure when a stepfamily is formed. They have to deal with a very uncertain situation. A new relationship (the repartnering parent and the new step-parent) is being formed that could potentially threaten the old cooperative parenting relationship. As in all new and ambiguous situations, it helps to have clearly defined roles. The repartnering parent needs to be clear about the role of the new partner with the children and where this role fits or overlaps with that of the children's other parent. The new partners need to agree on this and make sure that the role is a realistic one for a cooperative parenting situation. When the other parent experiences the new step-parent as supportive of their role, it is more than likely that they will be able to relax and deal with the children's transition difficulties in a productive and creative manner.

Having reached the end of this book, I am more convinced than ever that, if parents focus on their children's interests in separation, this will ultimately be in their own best interests too. This may be hard for parents to imagine initially. Yet, if we take a closer look at what parents have to do to focus on their children's interests, we see that they need to come to terms with the end of their marriage or relationship. This in turn allows them to rebuild their lives. If they focus on their own interests instead of those of their children, or try to cut across their former partner's interests, they remain embroiled in their relationship and inevitably end up feeling victimised. Children are caught in the middle and parents remain miserable and unfulfilled.

Children have a much better chance of leading satisfying and happy lives when their parents cooperate. But there is a spin-off in this for parents—parents are happier when their children are thriving and they don't have to deal with problematic behaviour. There is a better chance of achieving this situation if parents are not at loggerheads with the other parent, and there is also less risk of children developing severe problems.

So, even if the going is tough in the short term, it is worth persevering because, in the long term, there are demonstrable benefits for both adults and children. Cooperative parenting is a happier way forward.

Notes

Chapter One

1 Pryor, J. and Rodgers, B. (2001) *Children in Changing Families. Life After Parental Separation.* Oxford: Blackwell
2 Esping-Andersen, G., Gallie, D., Hemerijck, A and Myles, J, (2001) 'A New Welfare Architecture for Europe', submitted to the Belgian Presidency of the European Union, Leuven, October
3 Thompson, R.A. and Wyatt, J.M. (1999) 'Values, Policy and Research on Divorce', in *The Postdivorce Family: Children, Parenting and Society*, Thousand Oaks: Sage

Chapter Two

1 Edgar, D. (1999) *Men, Mateship and Marriage. Exploring Macho Myths and the Way Forward.* Sydney: HarperCollins: p. 313

2 Rodgers, B. and Pryor, J. (1998) *Divorce and Separation: The Outcomes for Children*. York: Joseph Rowntree Foundation: p. 52
3 Pryor, J. and Rodgers, B. (2001) *Children in Changing Families. Life After Parental Separation*. Oxford: Blackwell
4 O'Quigley, A. (2000) *Listening to Childen's Views*, York: Joseph Roundtree Foundation: p. 25
5 Dunn, J. and Deater-Deckard, K. (2001) *Children's Views of their Changing Families*. York: Joseph Rowntree Foundation: p. 18
6 Pryor, J. and Rodgers, B. (2001) *Children in Changing Families. Life After Parental Separation*. Oxford: Blackwell: p. 118–19
7 Wallerstein, J.S. and Kelly, J.B. (1980) *Surviving The Breakup*. New York: Basic Books: p. 35
8 ibid.: p. 42–9
9 NSA (National Stepfamily Association) (1999) *Children and Young Peoples Project—General Findings to Date*. London: National Stepfamily Association
10 Dunn, J. and Deater-Deckard, K. (2001) *Children's Views of their changing Families*. York: Joseph Rowntree Foundation
11 Ainsworth, M.D.S., Blehar, M.C., Waters, E. and Wall, S. (1978) *Patterns of Attachment: A Psychological Study of the Strange Situation*. Hillsdale, NJ: Erlbaum
12 Rodgers, B. and Pryor, J. (1998) *Divorce and Separation. The Outcomes for Children*. York: Joseph Rowntree Foundation: pp. 4–5
13 ibid.: pp. 4–5
14 Hetherington, M. and Kelly J. (2002) *For Better or Worse: Divorce Reconsidered*. London and New York: W.W. Norton and Co.: p. 229
15 ibid.
16 Rodgers, B. and Pryor, J. (1998) *Divorce and Separation. The Outcomes for Children*. York: Joseph Rowntree Foundation: p. 46
17 Pryor, J. and Rodgers, B. (2001) *Children in Changing Families. Life After Parental Separation*. Oxford: Blackwell: p. 73
18 Kelly, J. (1997) 'Children's post divorce adjustment: Research updates and implications for practice' Paper Presentation: Family Mediation—Beyond Divorce. Fourteenth Annual Conference of the Academy of Mediators quoted in 'Child Inclusive Practice in Family and Child Counselling and Family and Child Mediation', Report by Strategic Partners, commissioned by Commonwealth Attorney General's Department, Canberra

19 Amato, P. and Keith, B. (1991) 'Parental Divorce and the Well-being of Children: A Meta-analysis', *Psychological Bulletin*, Vol. 110, pp. 26–46

20 Stewart, A.J., Copeland, A.P., Chester, N.L., Malley, J.E. and Barenbaum, N.B. (1997) *Separating Together*. London and New York: The Guilford Press

21 Hetherington, M. and Kelly J. (2002) *For Better or Worse: Divorce Reconsidered*. London and New York: W.W. Norton and Co.: p. 127

22 ibid.: pp. 130–1

23 Australian Bureau of Statistics (1998) *Family Characteristics*, Canberra, April

24 Pryor, J. and Rodgers, B. (2001). *Children in Changing Families. Life After Parental Separation*. Oxford: Blackwell: p. 137

25 Amato, P. R. and Gilbreth, J. (1999) 'Non-Resident Fathers and Children's Well-being: A Meta-analysis' in *The Journal of Marriage and the Family*, Vol. 61: pp. 557–73

26 Smyth, B. and Weston, R. (2000) 'Financial Living Standards After Divorce: A Recent Snapshot', Research Paper No. 23, AIFS, Melbourne

27 Pryor, J. and Rodgers, B. (2001) *Children in Changing Families. Life After Parental Separation*. Oxford: Blackwell: p. 137

28 Esping-Andersen, G., Gallie, D., Hemerijck, A. and Myles, J. (2001) *A New Welfare Architecture for Europe*, submitted to the Belgian Presidency of the European Union, Leuven, October

29 Cowan, P.A. and Cowan, P.C. (1998) 'Assessing and Intervening with the Couple: A Research and Intergenerational Perspective'. Paper presented at Tavistock Marital Institute Conference: *Towards Secure Marriages; New Directions in Couple Research and Marriages*

30 Ricci, I. (1980) *Mum's House—Dad's House: Making Shared Custody Work*. London: Collier-McMillan

31 Bradshaw, J., Stimson, C., Skinner, C. and Williams, J. (1999) *Absent Father?* London and New York: Sage

32 Pryor, J. and Rodgers, B. (2001) *Children in Changing Families. Life After Parental Separation*. Oxford: Blackwell: p. 69

33 ibid.

34 Dunn, J. and Deater-Deckard, K. (2001) *Children's Views of their Changing Families*. York: Joseph Rowntree Foundation: p. 22

Chapter Three

1 Simpson, B., McCarthy, P. and Walker, J. (1995) *Being There: Fathers After Divorce.* Newcastle on Tyne: Relate Centre For Family Studies.
2 Lund, M. (1987) 'The Non-Custodial Father: Common Challenges in Parenting After Divorce' in Lewis, C. and O'Brien, M. (eds) *Reassessing Fatherhood.* Sage: London
3 Maccoby, E.E. Depner, C, and Mnookin, R.H. (1990) 'Co-parenting in the Second Year After Divorce', *Journal of Marriage and the Family*, Vol. 52, No. 1: pp. 141–5
4 Smart, C., Wade, A. and Neale, B. (2000) 'New Childhoods: Children and Co-parenting After Divorce', Children 5–16 Research Briefing, No. 7, ESRC
5 ibid.
6 Ahrons, C. (1995) *The Good Divorce.* New York: Harper Perennial: p. 163
7 Wallerstein, J.S. and Kelly, J.B. (1980) *Surviving The Breakup.* New York: Basic Books: p. 21
8 Simpson, B., McCarthy, P. and Walker, J. (1995) *Being There: Fathers After Divorce.* Newcastle on Tyne: Relate Centre for Family Studies
9 Kruk, E. (1992) 'Psychological and Structural Factors Contributing to the Disengagement of Noncustodial Fathers After Divorce' in *Family and Conciliation Courts Review*, Vol. 30, No. 1: pp. 81–101
10 Simpson, B., McCarthy, P. and Walker, J. (1995) *Being There: Fathers After Divorce.* Newcastle on Tyne: Relate Centre For Family Studies
11 ibid.
12 Smart, C. and Neale, B. (1999) *Family Fragments.* Cambridge: Polity
13 Lamb, M.E. (1999) 'Non-Custodial Fathers and their Impact', in Thompson, R. and Amato, P.R. (eds) *The Post Divorce Family.* London and New Delhi: Sage Publications: pp. 116–25
14 Hetherington, M. and Kelly J. (2002) *For Better or Worse: Divorce Reconsidered.* London and New York: W.W. Norton and Co.: p. 134
15 Smyth, B., Sheehan, G. and Fehlberg, B. (2001) 'Post-divorce Parenting patterns' in *Family Matters*, Australian Institute of Family Studies, No. 59, winter: pp. 61–3

Chapter Four

1 Roe, J. (1983) 'The End is Where We Start From: Women and Welfare since 1901' in Baldock, C. and Cass, B., *Social Welfare and The State*. Sydney: Allen and Unwin
2 Sanson, A. and Wise. S. (2001) 'Children and Parenting: The Past Hundred Years' in *Family Matters*, Australian Institute of Family Studies, No. 60, spring/summer
3 Moloney, L. (2000) 'Child Focused Parenting After Separation: Socio-Legal Developments and Challenges' in *Australian and New Zealand Journal of Family Therapy*. Vol. 21. No. 2: pp. 61–72
4 Spock, B. (1946) *The Common Sense Book of Bay and Childcare*. New York: Duell, Sloan and Pearce
5 Hetherington, M. and Kelly J. (2002) *For Better or Worse: Divorce Reconsidered*. London and New York: W.W. Norton and Co.: pp. 240
6 Nock, S. (1998) *Marriage in Men's Lives*. New York and Oxford: Oxford University Press
7 Morrow, V. (1998) *Understanding Families; Children's Perspectives*. London: National Children's Bureau
8 Smart, C. and Neale, B. (1999) *Family Fragments*. Cambridge: Polity Press
9 Sanson, A. and Wise, S. (2001) 'Children and Parenting: The Past Hundred Years' in *Family Matters*, Australian Institute of Family Studies, No. 60 spring/summer.
10 ibid.
11 Neale, B. and Smart, C. (1998) 'Agents or Dependants? Struggling to Listen to Children in Family Law and Family Research' Working Paper No. 3, Centre for Research on Family, Kinship, and Childhood, Leeds University: p. 26

Chapter Five

1 Cowan, P. A. and Cowan, P. C. (1998) 'New Families and Modern Couples as New Pioneers', in Mason, M.A., Skolnick, A. and Sugarman, S.D. (eds) *All Our Families: New Policies For A New Century*. New York: Oxford University Press: pp. 169–92

2 Nock, S. (1998) *Marriage in Men's Lives*. New York and Oxford: Oxford University Press: p. 133
3 ibid.: p. 61
4 McDonald, P. (2000) 'Gender Equity, Social Institutions and the Future of Fertility' in *Journal of Population Research*, Vol. 17, No. 1: pp. 1–16
5 Backett, K. (1997a) 'The Negotiation of Fatherhood', in Lewis, C. and O'Brien, M. (eds) *Reassessing Fatherhood*, London: Sage
6 de Singly, F. (1993) 'The Social Construction of a New Paternal Identity' in *Fathers of Tomorrow*, Denmark Ministry of Social Affairs, Conference Report: pp. 42–76
7 Smart, C. and Neale, B. (1999) *Family Fragments?* Cambridge: Polity Press
8 Orbach S. (1995) 'A Woman's Place?', in Curlow, C. (ed.) *Women, Men, and Marriage*. London: Sheldon
9 Tannen, D. (1990) *You Just Don't Understand: Women and Men in Conversation*. New York: William Morrow and Co.
10 Orbach S. (1995) 'A Woman's Place?', in Curlow, C. (ed.) *Women, Men, and Marriage*. London: Sheldon
11 James, K. (2001) 'Making Connections: Working With Males in Families', in Pease, B. and Camillieri, P. *Working with Men in Human Services*. Sydney: Allen and Unwin
12 Edgar D. (1999) *Men, Mateship and Marriage: Exploring Macho Myths and the Way Forward*. Sydney: HarperCollins: p. 302
13 Hetherington, M. and Kelly J. (2002) *For Better or Worse: Divorce Reconsidered*. London and New York: W.W. Norton and Co.: p. 26

Chapter Six

1 Seltzner, J.A. (1991b) 'Relationships Between Fathers and Children who Live Apart: The Father's Role After Separation' in *The Journal of Marriage and the Family*, Vol. 53: pp. 79–101
2 Meyer, D. (1999) 'Compliance with Child Support Orders in Paternity and Divorce Cases', in Thompson, R.A. and Amato, P.R. *The Post-divorce Family; Parenting, Children and Society*. Thousand Oaks: Sage
3 Smyth, B., Sheehan, G. and Fehlberg, B. (2001) 'Post-divorce Parenting Patterns' in *Family Matters*, Australian Institute of Family Studies, No. 59, winter: pp. 61–3

4 Bradshaw, J., Stimson, C., Skinner, C. and Williams, J. (1999) *Absent Father?* London and New York: Sage
5 Fehlberg, B. and Smyth, B. (2000) 'Child Support and Parent Child Contact', in *Family Matters*, Australian Institute of Family Studies, No. 57, spring/summer: pp. 20–6
6 Ahrons, C. (1995) *The Good Divorce*. New York: Harper Perennial
7 Therborn, G. (1993) 'The Politics of Childhood: The Rights of Children in Modern Times', in Castles, F. G. (ed.) *Families of Nations*. Dartmouth: Aldershot
8 Neale, B. and Smart, C. (2001) *Good to Talk*, Young Voice
9 Seddon, E. and Disney, H. (2000) 'It's Not All Over—Families After Separation and Divorce', Social Policy Research Centre, Collected Papers, University of New South Wales
10 O'Quigley, A. (2000) *Listening to Childen's Views*. York: Joseph Roundtree Foundation
11 Pryor, J. and Rodgers, B. (2001) *Children in Changing Families. Life After Parental Separation*. Oxford: Blackwell: p. 114

Chapter Seven

1 Moloney, L. (2000) 'Child Focused Parenting After Separation: Socio-Legal Developments and Challenges' in *Australian and New Zealand Journal of Family Therapy*, Vol. 21, No. 2: pp. 61–72
2 Ricci, I. (1980) *Mom's House—Dad's House: Making Shared Custody Work*. London: Collier McMillan
3 Ahrons, C. (1995) *The Good Divorce*. New York: Harper Perennial
4 Vaughan, D. (1990) *Uncoupling*. New York: Vintage Book: pp. 127–38
5 ibid.: pp. 139–52
6 Kubler-Ross, E. (1969) *On Death and Dying*. New York: McMillan
7 Folberg, J. and Taylor, A. (1984) *Mediation: A Comprehensive Guide to Resolving Conflict Without Litigation*. San Francisco: Jossey-Base: p. 7
8 Ahrons, C. (1995) *The Good Divorce*. New York: Harper Perennial: p. 144
9 Fisher, R. and Ury, W. (1981) *Getting to Yes*. Boston: Houghton-Miffin
10 Stone, D., Patton, B. and Heen, S. (1999) *Difficult Conversations: How to Discuss What Matters Most*. New York: Penguin
11 Ahrons, C. (1995) *The Good Divorce*. New York: Harper Perennial

12 Smart, C. and Neale, B. (1999) *Family Fragments?* Cambridge: Polity Press
13 Smart, C. and Wade, A. (2000) 'New Childhoods: Children and Co-parenting After Divorce', Children 5–6 Research Briefing, No. 7, ESRC

Chapter Eight

1 Ahrons, C. (1995) *The Good Divorce.* Harper Perennial: New York, p. 155
2 Johnston, J.R. (1993) 'Children Who Refuse Visitation', in Depner, C.E. and Bray, J.H. *Non-Residential Parenting.* Newberry Park: Sage
3 Wheelan, T. and Kelly, S. (1986) *A Hard Act to Follow.* Melbourne: Penguin
4 Bray, J.H. and Kelly, J. (1998) *Stepfamilies: Love, Marriage and Parenting in the First Decade.* New York: Broadway
5 Fern, E. and Small, K. *Step Parenting in the 1990s.* York: Joseph Rowntree Foundation
6 Bray, J.H. and Kelly, J. (1998) *Stepfamilies: Love, Marriage and Parenting in the First Decade.* New York: Broadway

References

Ainsworth, M.D.S., Blehar, M.C., Waters, E. and Wall, S. (1978) *Patterns of Attachment: A Psychological Study of the Strange Situation*. Hillsdale, NJ: Erlbaum

Ahrons, C. (1995) *The Good Divorce*. New York: Harper Perennial

Amato, P. and Keith, B. (1991) 'Parental Divorce and the Well-being of Children: A Meta-analysis' in *Psychological Bulletin*, 110: 26–46

Amato, P. R. and Gilbreth, J. (1999) 'Non-Resident Fathers and Children's Well-being: A Meta-Analysis' in *The Journal of Marriage and the Family*, Vol. 61, No. 557.573

Australian Bureau of Statistics (1998) *Family Characteristics*, Canberra, April 1997, Cat. No. 44420

Backett, K. (1997a) 'The Negotiation of Fatherhood' in Lewis, C. and O'Brien, M. (eds) *Reassessing Fatherhood*, London: Sage

Bradshaw, J., Stimson, C., Skinner, C. and Williams, J. (1999) *Absent Father*. London and New York: Sage

Bray, J. H. and Kelly, J. (1998) *Stepfamilies: Love, Marriage and Parenting in the First Decade*. New York: Broadway

Cowan, P.A. and Cowan, P.C. (1998a) 'Assessing and Intervening with the Couple: A Research and Intergenerational Perspective'. Paper presented at Tavistock Marital Institute Conference: *Towards Secure Marriages; New Directions in Couple Research and Marriages*

Cowan, P. A. and Cowan, P.C. (1998b) 'New Families and Modern Couples as New Pioneers' in Mason, M.A., Skolnick, A., and Sugarman, S.D. (eds), *All Our Families: New Policies For A New Century*. New York: Oxford University Press: 169–192

de Singly, F. (1993) 'The Social Construction of a New Paternal Identity' in *Fathers of Tomorrow.* Denmark Ministry of Social Affairs, Conference Report: 42–76

Dunn, J. and Deater-Deckard, K. (2001) *Children's Views of their Changing Families*. York: Joseph Rowntree Foundation

Edgar, D. (1999) *Men, Mateship and Marriage. Exploring macho myths and the way forward.* HarperCollins Publisher

Esping-Andersen, G., Gallie, D., Hemerijck, A. and Myles, J. (2001) A *New Welfare Architecture for Europe?* Submitted to the Belgian Presidency of the European Union, Leuven, October

Fern, E. and Small, K. (1999) *Steparenting in the 1990's*. York: Joseph Rowntree Foundation

Fisher, R. and Ury. W. (1981) *Getting to Yes*. Houghton-Miffin: Boston

Folberg, J. and Taylor, A. (1984) *Mediation: A Comprehensive Guide to Resolving Conflict without Litigation*. San Francisco: Jossey-Base

Hetherington, M. and Kelly J. (2002) *For Better or Worse: Divorce Reconsidered.* London and New York: W.W. Norton and Co.

James, K. 'Making Connections: Working With Males in Families' in Pease, B. and Camillieri, P. (2001) in *Working with Men in the Human Services*. Sydney: Allen and Unwin

Johnston, J.R. (1993) 'Children who Refuse Visitation' in Depner, C. E. and Bray, J.H. *Non-Residential Parenting*. Newberry Park: Sage

Kelly, J. (1997) 'Children's Post Divorce Adjustment: Research updates and implications for practice' Paper Presentation: Family Mediation—Beyond Divorce. Fourteenth Annual Conference of the Academy of Mediators. Quoted in Child Inclusive Practice in Family and Child Counselling and Family and Child Mediation, report by Strategic Partners, Commonwealth Attorney General's Dept.

Kelly, J. (2000) 'Children's Adjustment in Conflicting Marriage and Divorce: A decade review of research' in *Journal of the American Academy of Child Adolescent Psychiatry.* 39, (8): 963–97

Kruk, E. (1992) ' Psychological and Structural Factors Contributing to the Disengagement of Noncustodial Fathers After Divorce', *Family and Conciliation Courts Review.* 30, (1): 81–101

Lamb, M.E. (1999) 'Non-Custodial Fathers and Their Impact' in Thompson, R. and Amato, P.R. (eds) *The Post Divorce Family*, London and New Delhi: Sage Publications: 116–125

Lund, M. (1987) 'The Non-Custodial Father: Common Challenges in Parenting After Divorce' in Lewis, C. and O'Brien, M. (eds) *Reassessing Fatherhood.* London: Sage

Lynch, I. (2000) 'Trends in and Consequences of Investments in Children' in S. Danziger and Waldvogel (eds) *Securing the Future. Investing in Children from Birth.* New York: Russel Sage: 19–46

Lyon, C.M., Surrey, E. and T. and Judith, E. (1998) *Effective Support Services for Children and Young People when Parental Relationships Breakdown. A Child-Centred Approach.* Liverpool: University of Liverpool

Maccoby, E.E., Depner, C. and Mnookin, R. H. (1990) 'Co-parenting in the Second Year After Divorce', *Journal of Marriage and the Family*, 52, (1): 141–5

McDonald, P. (2000) 'Gender equity, social institutions and the future of fertility', *Journal of Population Research.* 17, (1): 1–16

Orbach S. (1995) 'A Woman's Place?' In Curlow, C. (ed). *Women, Men, and Marriage,* London: Sheldon

Meyer, D. (1999) 'Compliance with Child Support Orders in Paternity and Divorce Cases', in Thompson, R. A. and Amato, P.R. *The Postdivorce Family: Parenting, Children and Society.* Thousand Oaks: Sage

Moloney, L. (2000) 'Child Focused Parenting after Separation: Socio-Legal Developments and Challenges' in *Australian and New Zealand Journal of Family Therapy.* 21, (2): 61–72

NSA (National Stepfamily Association) (1999) *Children and Young Peoples Project—General Findings to Date*, National Stepfamily Association: London

Neale, B. and Smart, C. (1998) *Agents or Dependants? Struggling to Listen to Children in Family Law and Family Research.* Working Paper No.3, Centre for Research on Family, Kinship, and Childhood, Leeds University

Neale, B. and Smart, C. (2001) *Good to Talk,* Young Voice

Nock, S. (1998) *Marriage in Men's Lives.* New York and Oxford: Oxford University Press

O'Quigley, A. (2000) *Listening to Childen's Views.* York: Joseph Roundtree Foundation

Pryor, J. and Rodgers, B. (2001) *Children in Changing Families. Life After Parental Separation.* Oxford: Blackwell

Ricci, I. (1980) *Mom's House—Dad's House: Making Shared Custody Work.* London: Collier-McMillan

Rodgers, B. and Pryor, J. (1998) *Divorce and Separation. The Outcomes for Children.* York: Joseph Roundtree Foundation

Roe, J. (1983) 'The End is Where We Start From: Women and Welfare Since 1901' in Baldock, C..and Cass, B. *Social Welfare and The State.* Sydney: Allen and Unwin

Sanson, A. and Wise. S. (2001) 'Children and Parenting: The Past Hundred Years', in *Family Matters.* Australian Institute of Family Studies, 60, Spring/Summer: 36–45

Seddon, E. and Disney, H. (2000) 'It's Not All Over—Families After Separation and Divorce', Social Policy Research Centre, Collected Papers, University of New South Wales

Seltzner, J.A. (1991b) 'Relationships Between Fathers and Children Who Live Apart: The Father's Role After Separation', in *The Journal of Marriage and the Family,* 53: 79–101

Simpson, B., McCarthy, P. and Walker, J. (1995) *Being There: Fathers After Divorce.* Newcastle on Tyne: Relate Centre For Family Studies

Smart, C. and Neale, B. (1999) *Family Fragments?* Cambridge: Polity Press

Smart, C., Wade, A. and Neale, B. (2000) 'New Childhoods: Children and Co-parenting After divorce', Children 5–16 Research Briefing, No 7. E.S.R.C. Stirling, UK

Smith, A. B., Taylor, N, J., Gollop, M., Gaffney, M., Gold, M. and Henegan, M. (1997) *Access and Other Post-Separation Issues.* Dunedin, New Zealand: Children's Issues Centre

Smyth, B., Sheeham, G. and Fehlborg, H. (2001) 'Post-divorce Parenting Patterns', *Family Matters,* Australian Institute of Family Studies, No. 59, Winlov: 61–3

Smyth, B. and Weston, R. (2000) 'Financial Living Standard After Divorce: A Recent Snapshot', Research Paper. No. 23. Australian Institute of Family Studies, Melbourne

Spock, B. (1946) *The Common Sense Book of Bay and Childcare*. New York: Duell, Sloan and Pearce

Stewart, A.J., Copeland, A.P., Chester, N.L., Malley, J.E., and Barenbaum, N.B. (1997) *Separating Together.* London and New York: The Guilford Press

Stone, D., Patton, B. and Heen, S. (1999) *Difficult Conversations: How to Discuss What Matters Most*. New York: Penguin

Tannen, D. (1990) *You Just Don't Understand: Women and Men in Conversation*. New York: William Morrow and Co.

Therborn, G. (1993) 'The Politics of Childhood: The Rights of Children in Modern Times', in Castles F.G. (ed.) *Families of Nations*. Dartmouth: Aldershot

Thompson, R.A. and Wyatt, J.M. (1999) 'Values, Policy and Research on Divorce', in *The Postdivorce Family: Children, Parenting and Society.* Thousand Oaks: Sage

Vaughan, D. (1990) *Uncoupling*. New York: Vintage Books

Wallerstein, J.S. and Kelly, J.B. (1980) *Surviving The Breakup*. New York: Basic Books

Wheelan, T. and Kelly, S. (1986) *A Hard Act to Follow*. Melbourne: Penguin

Index